Hidden Pathways

A Travel Memoir

by
David Eaton

By the same author:
"I'm not a great lover of vicars"
Tom and Emma

Grandad Dave stories
Lowell catches a train
Brooke goes to the seaside
Bonnie goes to see the hens
Emmy goes to the fair

Way House Books

Front cover: The walkway at Finlaggan, the home of the Lords of the Isles.
(See page 85 and following.)

Hidden Pathways
A Travel Memoir

by
David Eaton

David Eaton has spent much of his life being a Parish Priest. In 2019, with his wife Ginny, he travelled by rail and sea to the west coast of Scotland and visited the Inner Hebrides, taking the Road to the Isles. What began as a holiday turned into a pilgrimage as he discovered the divine and sacred hidden in the people, places and the faith he found there.

WAY HOUSE BOOKS

Hidden Pathways
by David Eaton

Published in the United Kingdom by
Way House Books
Two Way House
Wheelers Lane
Brockham, Betchworth
Surrey RH3 7LA

ISBN: 978-0-9572965-2-7

First Published 2022

Designed by Andrew Dorman
andrew.dorman@btinternet.com

Printed by Short Run Press
www.shortrunpress.co.uk

Illustrations by the author unless otherwise attributed

For Ginny
In thanksgiving
for being my travelling companion
for more than fifty years
and making my life complete

Acknowledgements

I am grateful to Bob and Jenny Reid for their generous and comfortable hospitality in Dunoon, for showing us the sites and for being able to draw extensively from Bob's understanding of life in Cowal. Bob has generously shared both his historical research and also his own life and times for inclusion in this book.

I am also grateful to my friends and colleagues Bob Dickinson, Nick Sagovsky and Colin Tickner for reading a draft of the manuscript and their constructive feedback. In addition special thanks go to Bradley Langton and Rail Advent, Scotrail, RSPB Islay, Norrie Gilliland, Bloodaxe Books, Mairead Mackechnie and The Finlaggan Trust, Dan Romani and The Faith in Cowal website for permission to use material within their copyright and to Tessa Eley for capturing Donald so well on the train to Glasgow. And also to Rosemary Fletcher and The Happy Farmer for their friendly hospitality and allowing me to quote from Rosemary's Blog and to picture the man himself.

Thanks go to the Revd Keith Pagan for welcoming us to St Columba's and for pointing me in the right direction about The Scottish Episcopal Church, and to the Revd James Macfarlane for allowing me to recall the conversation we shared together. Sincere thanks to Debra Andrew-Cowen and for her memories of David Oliver and his unique contribution to church music.

I am also more than grateful to my editor Elizabeth Dobson for her generosity, guidance, good eye for detail and the time and trouble she took over the script. Also sincere thanks to Andrew Dorman for his design input and equal generosity in taking the text on board, coping with too many changes and for recommending Elizabeth to me.

Most especially my thanks also go to my wife Ginny, who made this journey with me and, in our Golden Wedding Anniversary year, for the journey we have shared in together over the last fifty years.

David Eaton
Brockham
2021

Contents

Introduction

The Kingdom of Heaven is like treasure which a man found hidden in a field. He buried it again, and in joy went and sold everything he had, and bought that field.
Matthew 13:44

Many things are hidden in our lives and the lives of the people we meet and the places we visit. Secrets are always hidden; in family life it is often what matters most that is never talked about, for shame and sometimes for modesty. We hide away from the challenges and changes of life which God brings to our door and we find hard to face up to. The vegetable seeds I sow on my allotment, which have the genesis of life hidden within their plain and crusty shells, are a metaphor for the lives we live; hidden within all of us is potential which often gets overlooked and neglected but which longs to germinate and blossom and yield a rich harvest. We travel many pathways in a lifetime which have new discoveries hidden within them.

People of faith believe that God is hidden but waiting to be discovered. That's why life is at best a pilgrimage and the encounters we make on the journey are often sacred. He is hidden in the secrets of our hearts; in our relationships and circumstances; in the great events of history and in the commonplace of everyday. He is hidden in those challenges and changes we encounter if we dig deep enough; in our imaginations; in the natural world around us and in the pages of books sacred and sometimes profane. We find him hidden in the Bible and the story it tells as he is hidden in the bread and wine of Holy Communion received into faithful hands. His discovery can transform and bring hope in the face of adversity when there is darkness all around. His hiddenness has given women, children and men the strength and courage to live lives in disregard of themselves. To discover the hidden God is to release love into our lives and into our world. He is the treasure for which many have given all that they possess in order to follow him.

I follow you with all my heart
Your right hand shall hold me fast.
Psalm 63

Beginning

Making a journey can simply be about getting from A to B but journeys have a lot more to offer. This proved to be the case for the journey Ginny and I made to the west of Scotland. It was a journey of discovery. We discovered the background and history of the places we visited as well as what goes on today. We met people on the way and enjoyed them for who they were and where their lives touched ours, albeit for a short time. This journey also opened us to each other. It renewed our love and what we mean to each other, as journeys sometimes do. It made me reflect on my own journey, where I had come from, how faith fitted in and how it helped shape who I have become. It is these discoveries I have tried to put down on paper: a collection of encounters triggered by a Scottish journey and which these pages bring to life.

In the TV sitcom *Gavin and Stacey* there's a nice moment at the beginning of their relationship when Gavin says to Stacey "If you say it, I'll say it back". He wants to say he loves her but because he's nervous he can't come straight out with it. But when she says it he says it too.

I hope this journey of discovery will allow those who read it to "say it too" by seeing what is hidden for you and waiting to be discovered. And if that's the case it will enrich the love you share with others, whether that's romantic love or the love which good friendship also brings to the journeys we make together. I hope your discoveries will awaken new life within you wherever you may be on the journey of life.

Oh, and what about God? He's there sure enough in the places and people and encounters we make on our journey, as he's always present, but often hidden, in all that makes up our lives, and it's there we find him.

God loves us and enjoys us, and so he wills that we love him, and firmly trust him; and all shall be well.[4]
Julian of Norwich

Part One
Finding a faith that listens
to the world and to the heart

Opposite:
The door that banged shut

One: Leaving it all behind

I banged the door shut and turned the key in the lock. We're off. If we haven't got it, we haven't got it. If we have left the oven on it will stay on, we're off; to Scotland. There's a journey to be made and banging the door shut brings a sense of relief. We get into the car and head for the station. Lorraine, our neighbour, is giving us a lift. Thanks, Lorraine. We're going by train. I used to drive but it's too far now and I am too far over the hill. So it's Victoria and Euston and Virgin Trains all the way to Glasgow.

There is relief in leaving it all behind. I get cornered by that "to do" list that I keep writing out. All the things that there are to be done – day by day and week by week, or so I think. If you're like me they are written down on bits of paper and crossed off one by one. Each task is in its way a completion but also each in its way a nag. They keep life together, these lists, but they also keep egging you on: don't sit down, there's more to do, come on get on with it.

Go away... I'm on holiday.

For a couple of weeks the "to do" list can be set aside. For sure other tasks come on board – getting from here to there – but it's all short term and

Early Days with Mum and Dad.

immediate. Life is simpler and out of a suitcase. So here's relief and a future to be embraced and enjoyed for its own sake. We're off and we're on a roll.

"We" is Ginny and me, together now for fifty years. We're different: Ginny is out there, "come on let's go", up for an adventure, spend the money, give it away if needs be. She likes nothing better than a good cause and a march on the streets; to dance in the aisles and hang from the rafters. Me? I'm cautious, "let's think about it", don't be too hasty, a saver and sometimes dragging my feet. Adventure isn't really my thing. Ginny helps me to be more outgoing and still up for it. Which is a good deal better than being stick-in-the-mud and a stay-at-home, which might otherwise be the case. Together we seem to work and complement each other; at least, we like to think so and after fifty years it looks as though we're going to make a go of it.

Leaving for the first time

Leaving home for the first time at 21 had for me some of the same feeling of relief. I needed to get away. Home had been overprotective. I learnt later that when I left Mum had said to Dad that if he hadn't been so protective I might have stayed around. This reflects her own anger at the way he had played it and also her own sense of loss. The truth is they both found it hard to let me go as perhaps all parents do when the moment of parting comes. My mum stood on the doorstep and wept as I closed the garden gate behind me. Dad just couldn't understand what was happening. I was the only one – their only one – and here I was off into the great unknown, how could that be? I think they had hoped I would settle nearby and be around the corner, like they were from their parents, but that wasn't to be. Settled communities were becoming less common because travel was becoming easier and work wasn't always on the doorstep. The horizons were lifting. I was part of the baby boom generation and there were opportunities for us that weren't determined by war, or by social class in the way they had once been. So perhaps I was up for an adventure after all. Youth was on my side. In my early twenties I was off to discover the world and follow the yellow brick road.

They found this hard to grasp. To them I had given up a safe and secure job in a bank and for what? To join the Church and become a priest. It was just so outside their experience, it didn't make sense. My mum had gone to church, a bit, my dad not at all. Church for them was something others did. The clergy were for Dad part of the gentry. He had grown up in a rural setting where knowing your place was part of the deal. And in any case wasn't it a fantasy on my part, hadn't I just got religion and it would wear off? Wake up, life isn't like that, not for us. We are not the sort of people who go to church. It's a foreign country. Why would you? What on earth do you think you are doing?

When Laurie Lee left home he wrote about it in *As I Walked Out One Midsummer Morning*. He was heading for Spain with little else but his fiddle to go with him. *His* mother stood at the top of the bank in front of their house and raised "one gnarled red hand in farewell and blessing, not questioning why I went".[1] Laurie would return and so would I but now I was setting out and leaving it all behind. My Mum and Dad *did* question why I went and the answers were hard to find and understand. I don't think they wanted to hold me back but they found it difficult to let me go. A parting had to be made but I had a sense of guilt about leaving, leaving them. If I had had brothers or sisters it might have been different but because I was the only one I felt responsible about not being there. It was a feeling that lingered for some time.

My parents' lives had been deeply shaped by the Second World War. To those of us who came after it was an event in history and it was behind us. For them it had turned their lives upside down. It had been a trauma, a pandemic in its way, to endure and get through. My father had had a breakdown because of the threat of it all. He wasn't on the front line but in the Home Guard and a reserved occupation, yet the anxiety was more than he could manage. It carried for my Dad a sense of shame he couldn't talk about. It was one of the secrets of our family life I was only to discover after he died. For me in my twenties the Second World War hardly featured. Later it would, as I came to understand what had happened in the war, what it all meant and how it ran so deep for my parents' generation. It is why now I find military ceremonial moving and emotional. Then I didn't. I was seeking my own place in the world and setting off to make my fortune as Laurie Lee and countless next generations have always done.

I set off with God and hope in my heart on what was the road to ordination but paradoxically I would also discover that leaving behind all that I knew was harder than I thought. It was partly the guilt of the only child but it was also my own dependency on what was familiar. That didn't and couldn't emerge until the break had been made but I was homesick at times. It made me anxious, my father's shadow crossing my path. I was never a stiff upper lip kind of person. I wouldn't have wanted to admit it at the time, a secret best kept to myself, but home pulled me back and I found it hard to resist even though I deliberately set a course to do so.

I also wish now looking back that, although a parting had to be made, I had been closer to my parents at that time and that we had talked more, shared more. It was much later in life before I could recapture the love which they clearly had for me and I for them. This comes across in photographs which I have of when I was much younger, the three of us on holiday by the sea smiling and happy to be together (see page 16). As you can see I always was a snappy dresser! These are only holiday snaps but they show how precious those golden years are when children are young and you love and cherish them greatly for being just that; what I felt and feel for my own children and grandchildren. You can't believe the sweetness they hold and how it opens your heart. It's what every child needs and deserves as a sure foundation for adult life. There is something very humbling and affirming in realising that you also were the recipient of just such love and affection. Not all children, sadly and often tragically, receive love like this and when they don't it shows. Of course the time does come for leaving home but it doesn't and shouldn't have to mean an absence of love felt and expressed, a bond to go on sharing and to be enjoyed. I see that now. Love is a river that runs deep and long. That was true for my parents and the love they gave me, which has shaped so much of what came after, and is captured for me evocatively in those photographs.

I was leaving to widen my experience and to gain a greater resilience on the road to being ordained. Living at home and working locally wasn't going to do that. But I also came to see that it was important not to dismiss what I might really be feeling about myself, my parents and the journey I was making. That underlying bond of love meant everything. For me the best of being truly human is to be *both* strong and independent yet also sensitive in the sense of allowing myself to be vulnerable and willing to share and express that with others. So often it is doing just that which creates a bond and becomes a point of growth. When Jesus raised Lazarus from the tomb he took a strong initiative and effective leadership; he was tough minded. Yet in the story we also see a natural empathy with the sadness of bereavement. Jesus listens carefully to Mary and Martha and their feelings on the loss of their brother.

> *When Jesus therefore saw Mary weeping, and the Jews also weeping which came with her, he groaned in the spirit and was troubled. And he said, Where have ye laid him? They said unto him, Lord, come and see.*
> *Jesus wept.*
> *Then said the Jews, Behold, how he loved him.*[2]

Jesus was both strong and sensitive as he needed to be. A dynamic faith is one which finds the right gear for the right occasion and allows the feelings we have to surface and not be ashamed.

Euston

We arrive at Euston with time to kill and get into a comfortable station café. The busker is giving us a good rendition of Van Morrison covers so for once there is some not half bad music as well. You could always reckon on getting a newspaper at the station but now you can have morning coffee, lunch and dinner and do the whole of the weekly shop as well as get most of the presents for Christmas. There's a short queue in the café but the team behind the counter have a system: one takes the order and the dosh; the rest prepare the drinks and get the food and deliver it to you at the other end as you move along the counter. It works well except that she on the coffee machine has a strong wrist and bangs out the used coffee with lust and vigour. We settle at a table but the banging echoes through the building; bang, bang, bang – there she goes again. Ginny can't put up with this for long and threatens death or worse. It's time to move out to find our platform.

I reckon I have done a pretty good job with booking the tickets for this trip and hand out our printed copies so they can be scanned and get us through the gate and onto the platform. I also have them on the phone but I still don't trust these phones or know how to work them exactly. They lead you on a game of hide and seek about where they keep things and take pleasure in not letting you know. Old-school, I like to have something in my hand, a hard copy you can be sure about. The platform number goes up on the digital departures board – it's Platform 6. We make a dash with the rest of the crowd to find our train, following the backs and suitcases on wheels bobbing along in front of us. I don't know why the rush because the seats are booked. It's not as if we need to elbow our way to find good ones we like, but herd instinct has taken over as we surge forward.

On the train

We settle in our seats and the mobiles come out. Oh! There's a message from the surgery. I have recently had a blood test. These seem to be routine at my time of life.

The surgery is attentive and efficient. We consider ourselves fortunate to have a good GP surgery on our doorstep. Their recorded message says I should make a routine appointment with the GP. I grasp hold of that word *routine* and hang on to it. It's a life saver. It means, I think, that there is no threat of impending doom – something hidden and secret and awful that has suddenly come to light – or they would have said, surely, and I would be told to "get round here in double quick time". Despite this, anxiety now takes hold. We are old friends and health is one of the things that sets me off.

We are in a quiet carriage so I go out into the corridor to ring the surgery. Not that I can make an appointment: no diary and we are on the way to Scotland for goodness sake. But I can tell them this and try to get to speak to the GP. There's an answerphone message: the practice is closed today because there is an area meeting of all medical staff. I can wait, just. I must remember not to have blood tests before going away. Going away is enough on its own, thank you very much.

As I knew we would be on it I have brought with me a copy of *The Train to Glasgow* by Wilma Horsbrugh, which I first heard recited by Brian Cant on *Playaway* on BBC Children's television in the seventies. Brian has just the right pace and emphasis.

Here is the train to Glasgow
Here is the driver
Mr MacIver,
Who drove the train to Glasgow.

Here is the guard from Donibristle
Who waved his flag and blew his whistle
To tell the driver
Mr MacIver,
To start the train to Glasgow.

Here is a boy called Donald MacBrain,
Who came to the station to catch the train
But saw the guard from Donibristle
Wave his flag and blow his whistle
To tell the driver,
Mr MacIver,
To start the train to Glasgow.

The train to Glasgow: The Princess Elizabeth regularly ran on the west coast line into Glasgow main line station. *Bradley Langton/RailAdvent*

Here are the hens and here are the cocks,
Clucking and crowing inside a box,
In charge of the guard, that kindly man,
Who, at the last moment, hauled into the van
That fortunate boy called Donald MacBrain,
Who came to the station to catch the train
But saw the guard from Donibristle
Wave his flag and blow his whistle
To tell the driver,
Mr MacIver,
To start the train to Glasgow.

Here is the train. It gave a jolt,
Which loosened a catch and loosened a bolt,
And let out the hens and let out the cocks,
Clucking and crowing out of their box,
In charge of the guard, that kindly man,
Who at the last moment, hauled into the van
That fortunate boy called Donald MacBrain,
Who came to the station to catch the train
But saw the guard from Donibristle
Wave his flag and blow his whistle
To tell the driver,
Mr MacIver,
To start the train to Glasgow.

Now Donald was quick and Donald was neat
And Donald was nimble on his feet.
He caught the hens and he caught the cocks
And he put them back in their big box.
The guard was so pleased as pleased could be
And invited Donald to come for tea
On Saturday, at Donibristle,
And let him blow his lovely whistle,
And said in all his life he'd never
Seen a boy so quick and clever.

And so did the driver,
Mr MacIver,
Who drove the train to Glasgow.[3]

Donald, who was quick and neat. *Tessa Eley*

This is a poem that rises and falls like a good and happy jig as it tells its story. It is just fun to hear read out. It brings back the time when our children were young and we watched what have now become classics of children's television – *Bagpuss* and *Trumpton* and *Ivor the Engine. The Train to Glasgow* evokes in me much nostalgia which should have been put away long since but isn't. The reason I had brought it with me was to read it to Ginny. It was to be something to share together and cuddle up with, even on a train – *especially* on a train in this case. But so overtaken am I with "me" and all things to do with the surgery and health that I forget. On remembering later I give myself a cuff round the ear; it's not all about you, you know.

On this train to Glasgow we are sitting in a four with a table between us. The others are two young women who don't seem to know each other and are each preoccupied with their devices. Earphones in for one and laptop on the go for the other. This one types away rapidly at we know not what. The young have the power of attention and concentration in a busy place that left me long since *and* she types with all her fingers. I have brought a book to read on the journey all about where we are going, but, after the lettuce and cheese pitta bread we had for lunch, reading makes me feel queasy and I give up. This is partly brought on by the movement of the train. It used to take six hours from London to Glasgow but now it's four and a half. The price for this seems to be a good deal of rocking and rolling; the train doesn't slow down on the corners. The scenery goes up and down in the windows. It's like being at sea.

There is no scheduled stop until Lancashire: Preston, Wigan and then Carlisle. We had been to Wigan before on the way to Southport to visit a friend, who was sadly in a hospice there. There are two stations in Wigan close to each other; it's where you change for Southport. We had time to go into the local pub as we went from one station to the other. I couldn't understand what *they* said and they certainly couldn't understand what I said.

Saying goodbye

The friend we had gone to Southport to see was, like me, called David and he was my Director of Music and Organist when I was the Vicar. He had great musical gifts and was in his way unique in the role. He was equally at home with both classical and contemporary music. He was a composer, too, and had written inspiring and uplifting pieces of church music for choir and organ. There was something joyful and exuberant about his music. He also worked professionally for a well-known holiday camp and had achieved success in composing for their floor show and children's entertainment. But now he was dying from an aggressive cancer. He had had the available treatment but to no avail. He was to die prematurely in his fifties.

I have taken many funerals but not all stay with me. This would not be true for David. His was the tragic loss of someone who had a big creative potential and who died before this could be fully realised. He had hidden within him the music gene wanting to burst into flower and full of creative possibilities. When we lose someone we care about we can brush it under the carpet, pretend we are over it or that it didn't happen. We can pretend it doesn't hurt, when it does. We never forget.

So what *can* we do with these losses we encounter? One way is to carry them with us so that they are part of our journey still, but in a different way. They are no longer alongside us, those we love, but they are still part of us and their influence and presence will always be felt. We don't stop loving those who have died, we cherish and treasure them, our love for them remains and we have them always in our hearts.

Much earlier in life Ginny and I lost three babies in late pregnancy. We gave each a name because they were each a person in their own right. We didn't know them but they were part of us. Ginny, of course, remembers better than I do the pregnancies and the births, the details and the emotions, the precious things of each. It was she who carried them and gave birth to them bravely knowing they were unlikely to survive, these babies of ours. They remain part of us. We don't think of them a lot now but from time to time we do. Their loss has shaped us and changed our lives; not least because we adopted a baby daughter after it seemed unlikely we could have another live birth ourselves. We already had a son, Chris, and now Carly arrived at 10 weeks, hats in the air and joy in our hearts. Chris said: "Can we keep her?" and we did.

People ask, do you think of them differently, these children of yours? We don't. They are different because they are different people but in our hearts we cherish them just the same. They, and their growing families, have been with us for a while now. We travel together. There is a bond and a love as in any family and that's why when someone we care about dies it hurts; the bond is scarred. In our case the scars are with us not in pride or resentment but in hope. What happened has shaped us for the better. The loss has become part of the journey.

The ability to accept our losses and for them to become part of us depends on our being sensitive to our feelings. Feelings are scary, but bottled up they are also damaging; depression drives us down, anger lashes out. We leave people and places and they leave us. The leaving sometimes stirs hopeful expectation and sometimes sadness and trauma. It often involves loss and what we are to do with it. Denial and avoidance don't work; stoicism is overrated although courage will be needed. But if by one means or another these losses can be accepted and become part of who we are, we travel on, changed but often bigger people with more understanding of the suffering of others. Those we love "but see no longer" are always with us.

All this is why the crucifixion of Jesus matters so much and why it is at the centre of Christian faith. It is God's loss of a son, it is God suffering as all human beings suffer, it is a scar on the face of the divine. God enters the human experience of loss that we all encounter. He paid a great price for doing so. He even forgave those who made him suffer and because of this we see, in a way that cannot be doubted, that he is always with us and his way is the way of love.

> *Would you know your Lord's meaning in this? Learn it well. Love was his meaning. Hold fast to this, and you shall learn and know more about love... you will never need to know or understand about anything else for ever and ever. Thus did I learn that love was his meaning.*[4]

Glasgow Central and some of the 48,000 panes of glass.

Two: Glasgow in the age of steam and shipbuilding

We arrive at Glasgow Central Station on time but this station is not quite what I thought it would be. Its appearance is restrained and it doesn't shout at you like a modern high street does with its array of multiple outlets. What looks like the original nineteenth-century woodwork has been preserved. So instead of "Burger King" glowing in neon, the branding is up over their outlet but in restrained brass lettering on a dark wood background. It works rather well and introduces a sense of heritage not often associated with burgers. But it's fast food as we know and love it once you cross their threshold. The menus are up in lights for you to touch what you fancy and place the order which then emerges without a word being spoken. I keep going. The station also has a magnificent roof made up of over 48,000 pieces of glass. It is a Victorian building and retains its original Victorian atmosphere and dignity. It has an unexpected history as well.

This is well documented in *Glasgow's Forgotten Village* by Norrie Gilliland. The station was built in the days when the different railway companies were in daggers-drawn competition with each other. They were seen as good investment opportunities providing you backed the right horse in the race, in this case the best one to bring the railway into central Glasgow. Had the companies co-operated more the outcome would have been cheaper, given the high price of land. But in the end two stations were created: Central, by the Caledonian Railway Company, and Glasgow South Western Railway's St Enoch. These could almost certainly have been built on one site had the will been there to do so.

Where Glasgow Central now stands there had been a village called Grahamston, then on the outskirts of Glasgow. The middle and eastern parts of the village were razed to the ground to enable the railway to come in. This was in 1879 and the station was opened on 1 August. The rest of the village including the church of St Columba went the same way at the turn of the century as the station expanded. The village had about 600 residential and commercial occupiers, only 42 of whom are thought to have agreed to the development. When the City Architect gave evidence to a committee of enquiry he said: "Why in 1873 are we enquiring into station accommodation in Glasgow? For this reason, that the companies cannot agree, it all comes to that. It is the jealousy and mutual distrust which they have of one another which has driven the Glasgow Corporation here to oppose these Bills".[5]

According to the Network Rail website there is now a much praised tour of the station conducted by Paul Lyons, in a bowler hat and with a flowing long white beard, or his colleague Jackie Ogilvie. Paul is an enthusiast and a former Network Rail employee. It is due to his enthusiasm that these tours got going and have proved popular. The original idea for a tour came about during the 2013 Glasgow Open Doors Day. The station made 100 tickets available but received over 83,000 applications.

The BBC reported: "Such popularity for a station tour might seem unfathomable, until you consider the sheer number of people for whom Glasgow Central is part of their everyday lives."

"It's the busiest station this side of London," says Paul, with just a hint of pride. About 106,000 people pass through the station every day: to catch trains, to meet friends, to say long-awaited hellos and painful goodbyes. "It's more than a railway station," Paul explains. "It's part of the very social fabric of Glaswegians."

The guides take you below ground which reveals the station in an earlier incarnation and some of the village of Grahamston as well. The

Caledonian Railway Company left behind a lot of archive material which has been rediscovered. Mr Lyons gives an evocative commentary on the life of the station since its nineteenth-century creation. Part of what you see are earlier platforms which are now hidden and got the chop under Dr Robert Beeching's 1960s railway cutbacks. None of this is apparent to the travellers like us just passing through up above. It's all hidden from view below the present-day platforms: a secret waiting to be discovered and enjoyed for its own sake 150 years later. Next time we will allow more time and take the tour, which is acclaimed by some as the best in Scotland.

Port Glasgow

As it is, the next bit for us is to get to Dunoon, which sits on the other side of the Clyde estuary, so it's train to Gourock and then ferry across the water. The ticket takes in both and it's not long to wait. It's going-home time and the train is full of commuters. We don't get a seat but standing means we get a good view of the Clyde estuary which we pass on our right. The train is a "fast" and we don't stop at every station but at Port Glasgow we do. This was once a centre of shipbuilding for which the Clyde was world famous – and not only because it was on the Clyde Billy Connolly learnt his trade as

The sun setting over the Clyde *Shutterstock*

a welder. After the Second World War the sun was already setting over the Clyde and shipbuilding. There is still some shipbuilding on the Clyde, but not on the scale it was, when about a fifth of world shipping was launched into its chill waters and huge drag chains stopped the ships colliding with the far bank as they ran down the slipway.

It was to Port Glasgow that Stanley Spencer came as an official war artist in the Second World War, appointed by the War Artists' Advisory Committee. It wasn't in him to record the big grand moments of the shipbuilding world like a launch or a royal visit. Instead he goes, in typical Spencer fashion, for close-ups of the men at work who actually built the ships. These are spread out in a continuous array across his canvases: small cameos of this world of work so important to men and their identity. The work and the hard graft of making ships was for many hidden from view. Stanley puts it on full display for all to see and in doing so pays tribute to those who did it: take a good look, this is what it means to make ships which are the life blood of the nation. They defend our shores and export and import our food and goods.

The close-ups he paints are homely and intimate, as they are in the murals he painted for the First World War Memorial Chapel at Burghclere, which took him five years to complete. For these he drew on his own experience as a hospital orderly in Salonika in the First World War, highlighting tasks like bedmaking, brewing tea and filling water bottles. "People generally make a home for themselves wherever they are, and whatever their work", he wrote.[6] Home was always important for Stanley. That's why he travelled back to Cookham each night when he studied at the Slade in London. Home was reassuring and comforting. He knew the importance of the ordinary and everyday that holds life together. For the men who built ships on the Clyde it was as though their workplace was their home because they were at ease there, knew who they were and were confident of their ability to do the work asked of them.

In the way he portrays them Stanley prizes these men of Port Glasgow and the work they did caulking, welding, riveting, as riggers and plumbers and in laying the keel plate. That's why the passing of all the traditional industries in the years following the Second World War was always going to be fiercely resisted by the work force. It was never just a question of economics; the shipbuilding, mining and steel making industries gave identity to the men who worked in them. Stanley knew that and in his paintings he holds, values and cherishes what meant so much. When he painted them it looked as though it was a way of life and work that would go on for ever on the Clyde but that was not to be, and the loss of identity with its decline was heartbreaking.

Stanley is known for his religious paintings where he takes biblical scenes like the crucifixion and places them in his home village. He always described these as his serious work. In addition he painted what he called "pot boilers" which were often attractive countryside scenes and earned him some useful income. You can make much of Stanley Spencer's religious paintings and become too high flown in doing so. In them, as in the paintings he did in Port Glasgow, he is often simply recording his own life experience and the experience of men and women like him, more than making any kind of religious comment. It is *human* experience he captures by focusing on the life of Jesus. In his humanity Jesus stands in solidarity with ours.

This is why for Stanley it was his serious work. The everyday domestic and workplace tasks he knew so well made Stanley who he was and mattered for their own sake. In the life and death of Jesus we see who Jesus was through *his* work and relationships and encounters. They draw out his true identity and his significance is revealed. In his own home community of Cookham Stanley found God hidden and yet most real. It was here that Stanley was truly himself. It was the same for the people he painted and caught in time in Port Glasgow. This was their home, where they had grown up and where they were themselves; just as it was for Jesus of Nazareth

Stanley was a spiritual artist because he gives these everyday settings a transcendent quality. By drawing out the true nature of the people he painted, seen best in their work, the rough and ready world of the shipyard workers is transcended by their skill and dignity and commitment. In his Cookham paintings, by putting the Biblical stories of Jesus in his home village Stanley draws out the true nature of God. In Jesus humanity is seen at its best and so because of this he reveals the divine. The life of an ordinary man becomes transcendent and in him and through him we see God.

If men and women are made in the image and likeness of God then for the men ship building in Port Glasgow that likeness was found through the work they did, the identity it gave them and the fight they had for social justice and a fair deal in the workplace. God's presence may not have been obvious but all those things matter to God. The work was dirty and tough.

But if God isn't in those very places where *can* we find him? It is these places and experiences that are the backbone of people's lives. They are the key to who we are and who we become. Faith that is blind to that becomes trapped in a backwater away from all that is important in shaping people and the lives we live. It becomes holier than thou and irrelevant. The deeper truth is God is hidden in the ordinary and everyday landscapes of our lives waiting for us to discover him and to know he is on our side and always will be.

The Pilgrim Path

Three: Dunoon, going to school and coming to faith

At Gourock we leave the train and take a short walk to line up for the ferry which is on its way. It takes just under half an hour and Jen is waiting for us as we disembark. We have come to stay three nights with Jenny and Bob Reid who have lived in Dunoon, they tell us, for some fourteen years. Jen and Ginny were at secondary school together and have kept in touch. Bob was brought up in Dunoon and it works well for them now being close to family.

Their house is typically Scottish, having that very solid look which stone always brings. It was originally a bungalow but the roof space has been opened up with a TV and plenty of sitting and lounging space; lounging we like. The bedrooms are on the ground floor and the guest room is also very comfortable with its own en-suite. As we arrive Bob comes out the house to greet us which makes us feel welcome and at home – I make a note to stir myself and remember to do the same when we have guests. Get up and get out there for goodness sake.

Jenny and Bob are both retired like us but the grass doesn't grow under their feet. Jen volunteers at a refugee resettlement charity in Glasgow and has a good first-hand knowledge of what being a refugee really means. The debate at national level focuses on numbers but what Jenny sees is that refugees are people. They are not scroungers but human beings in sometimes desperate need. She has also been helping to organise a local jazz festival which has gone well and we are sorry to miss it. Bob has developed an interest in local history and will take us on a guided tour.

School days

But before all that we are soon into school days and "Do you remember..." and "Whatever happened to...". When Ginny arrived in Edinburgh in the early sixties Scotland was a very different place from today and certainly from the English south coast which is what she had left behind. In Scotland then, only men went into pubs and they were for drinking and not much else. Boys had always fought in playgrounds but, at the secondary school Ginny and Jenny went to, girls did it as well. Ginny benefited at first from being English in that she had a kind of novelty value and so was protected from any casual violence that might be on offer. This did not, of course, include the strap. This was carried by teachers over the shoulder. It was used to warm the hands of their pupils should there be any stepping out of line.

This kind of discipline reflects days when behaviour was enforced in a different kind of way from today. "A good leathering didn't do us any harm" was very much the ethic of the day. Not all the staff were of this frame of mind and their art teacher is remembered for being much more "one of us" and not using a strap. This may have been a qualification for getting the job as an art teacher. In my own secondary school, in the south, the art teacher married one of his pupils and so was definitely one of us. This unlikely match was always referred to in a whisper and behind the hand, hidden because it was like a crime had been committed, which for some it had.

I got a taste of school discipline in my first week at secondary school. There was a caning on stage in an assembly. The culprits had beaten up another pupil and broken his arm by throwing him into a ditch. The head was not best pleased, not to mention the victim, and made that plain by this public flogging. He wanted to put the fear of God into anyone else who might be tempted to do the same. He certainly succeeded with me, not that I was much into arm breaking or ditch throwing, let me say.

I had an even greater fear before arriving from primary school as a unsuspecting eleven-year-old. The rumour on the street had been that, after PE, showers were taken on a co-educational basis and boys and girls were all in together. At eleven this did put something like the fear of God into me and did not have the attraction it might have done when I was a few years older. Mercifully of course I needn't have worried.

Youth groups

The two girls in Edinburgh were part of a "Gang of Four" and after school they would invariably turn up at Ginny's house after raiding the pie shop opposite to stuff their faces in the way only teenagers know how. The local church was English Episcopal and a rarity in its own right. The incumbent was usually English and at that time was a good-looking and energetic young minister with a bike. He put his bike to good use and visited Ginny and her mum so that both were soon part of church life. Ginny joined the youth fellowship, along with the other members of the "Gang of Four". The church and the youth fellowship proved to be an anchor point in her teenage years and a doorway into faith. This is also an experience matched by my own. It is difficult to overestimate the influence that church youth groups had on the teenagers who went to them at this time.

Evangelicalism in the Church of England was then still the poor relation but it was beginning to emerge and be more significant. It now occupies centre stage and the reason is to be seen in these early youth fellowships of the sixties. They were lively and friendly places to be and hang out. They weren't slick or IT savvy as would be needed now, but they did manage to bridge the gap between the formality of church services and something more accessible and social for young people, even in a draughty church hall. Having friends is an important part of teenage life and church youth groups had this on offer. Evangelical Christians are good at mixing it with the culture of the day – walking the walk, talking the talk, playing the music. These, with friendship on tap, went a long way when you were setting out to find your way in the world. Here was a social grouping that wasn't family and represented a kind of early independence.

The youth fellowship was also for me an introduction to middle class life and living. My family had an artisan background. My dad had been brought up in Windsor Great Park where his father was a gamekeeper. My other grandfather was a cabinet maker. We didn't socialise a lot outside of the family. Church was a new world, a different world and it drew me in. I was never someone with bags of confidence to unpack but these middle class church people had a lot and I found it attractive and, make no mistake, I wanted to be part of it, part of them. At the end of a youth fellowship evening we would often go back to someone's house. We would watch *That Was The Week That Was*, the leading satirical show of the time on TV. I felt I had arrived.

Youth fellowships offered something to believe in for teenagers who were emerging into adult life and hungry for a philosophy to nail their colours to. Not everyone saw it like that and there were many who fell away from any kind of church involvement. But for both Ginny and myself it was this which held us to the faith and to the church. In 1945 the Church of England had published *Towards the Conversion of England* in memory of Archbishop William Temple who had died prematurely the year before. Converting England is the kind of aspiration which today even the most ardent would find it hard to put their name to, but then it seemed it might still be on and revival, or something like it, was just around the corner. Part of the rationale for this was what these youth fellowships had on offer. It was the case, as the report suggested, that young people were looking for a faith to believe in and that they didn't want anything watered down, the stronger the brew the better. In many a church youth fellowship this is just what could be found and I was pleased to be one of those who found it.

Conversion

It meant that in church youth groups around the country blood red conversion was high on the agenda and putting this in front of young people was at the heart of the programme. It meant an epilogue at the end of each evening, much praying behind the scenes and "getting alongside" members. This was an overused and sometimes loaded phrase at the time. The hope and hidden agenda was to bring young people to an act of commitment. The Billy Graham rallies of the fifties and sixties represented the epitome of how this worked. At these there was always an invitation from Billy to "get up out of your seat" and come to the front and come to Jesus.

All this worked for me and it was through the youth fellowship that I came to faith and it stuck. I didn't go forward with Billy but I did make an act of commitment kneeling beside my bed and it felt like a turning point. It felt like a relief to have done it, which may reflect some of the pressure I must have been under at the time, both from myself and from others as well as a desire to find a faith to live by.

Conversion is accepted in the world of religion, within Christianity as in other major world faiths. It begs some questions about manipulating other people even when the intention is genuine and there is real concern for people as people. Looking back now I do have some scepticism about what happened. Was I hoodwinked by the attractions of a social class that I hadn't known before, was I exploited by those who brought pressure to bear, was I naïve about life and faith and bought a package that had too many holes in it, was it the young and pretty girls that also went along that I was really drawn to? Some of all these things were at play but even so it got me started on a journey of faith I have been on ever since. God works with what he's got available. I don't regret making that commitment. It has enabled me to live life in a particular way and with a particular calling which has been fulfilling and satisfying. It has not all been plain sailing, of course, but the tight corners have often brought a depth to life, and faith, which has been enriching.

What faith gave me, and why I made an act of commitment kneeling beside my bed, was a way of understanding life. I was no longer without a reference point but had some way of knowing what life was about and how to meet it. It meant that God was there and I could speak to him and tell him all. He could speak to me in return. The Bible was the way he did it and so Bible reading and Bible study became a major preoccupation. I certainly put in some hours doing this on my own and with others in a regular Bible study group. I was a teenager and everything was black and white. The ethos of youth groups and Bible study groups fitted in well. Problems were easily resolved. Short and simple booklets were readily available dealing with supposed threats to belief like science, suffering and the problem of evil. You can see why my dad thought I had got religion; in many ways I had.

Moving on

What brings people to faith is often, as in my case, a combination of different factors and influences. Some will only be valid at the time, some will stand the test of time. My conversion was a good place to begin. It was genuine even if now looking back I have some qualifications about what happened. It was also a good place to move on from. What had worked well for a naïve teenager soon began to wear thin. It became clear that life wasn't black and white and that, because suffering and injustice were often at the heart of human experience, my faith needed reshaping. It became clear that hardline responses to moral and ethical issues didn't work either and something more open and big hearted was what I looked for. Change was on the way. It had to be, because an important aspect of faith, as of life, is growth and development. Stand still and you find yourself in a rut.

To begin with the message had to change. The message I had responded to was almost all about the death of Jesus. This is what was put across in those epilogues and whenever faith was talked of. Jesus had died for me on the cross. It meant that my sins could be forgiven. Sin was the problem and played well to teenage guilt: I deserved to die but all was well because Jesus died in my place. My sin and guilt make God angry but the death of Jesus appeases his anger and I can walk free. I am forgiven. In most teenage minds of the day sin was about sex. Forgiveness laid that to rest, or you hoped it did, all those wild teenage fantasies and skirmishes that were too embarrassing to talk about. But did I really deserve to die? Was God really so angry that he needed to be placated to have his anger turned? What sort of God was it that put his own Son to death and that required a death, to love and to forgive. It gets very tortuous, this way of thinking. Something simpler and more straightforward was needed.

I am happy to admit to being a reactionary on this subject. When you move on and see things differently it is tempting to stamp your foot and bang the table when what you used to believe comes into view. So I find myself critical of those who hold this understanding of the death of Jesus that I used to have but have now grown out of, as I like to think. To see his death as something we deserved and he took upon himself to assuage God's anger doesn't do it for me now.

What I now think is God was loving from the beginning, it's who he is, he doesn't need transactions between heaven and earth to let that love show. It is his love which holds us and draws out our commitment and conversion. Let's have lashings of it in church life and in the life of the world. It speaks of a God who loves us, knows us by name and who stands in solidarity with all who suffer. In the death of his only son he too has suffered. Suffering is part of his creation and he is caught up in that as much as we are.

But the strange thing is that, whichever interpretation of the death of Jesus suits you best, maybe they end up in the same place.

There are those who believe (as I once did) "Christ died for me and took my place on the cross" and that he died to satisfy an angry God by his sacrifice. But it is this which shows just how much he loves us. The rivers of guilt and shame can run very deep. This interpretation postulates a legal transaction between God and humanity: a price or penalty is paid for sin committed, that price is not paid by us but by God. For some this may be a helpful model which releases them from their burden of guilt and I wouldn't want to undermine its appeal. Here the focus is on *our* problem of how to get free and that is a real concern for some.

Then there are those who (as I now do) see the death of Christ as an act of solidarity with the suffering of the world and a demonstration of his compassion when he forgave even those who nailed him to the cross. He suffered as we suffer. It was undeserved in him as it often is in us. His suffering is in solidarity with ours. What this teaches us is just how much God loves the world. He shares our shoes and knows what it means to suffer and to die. Because of this it is beyond any doubt that his love will ever leave us. Here the focus is on God and *his* motivation and character. No transactions are required; he is a forgiving God, that's what he's like.

If there is a difference between these two views it is in the contrasting pictures these two understandings give us of who God is. For me the first paints God in a poor light because it shows him as requiring something, a sacrifice, before he will speak to us. It makes God into a monster requiring the death of his Son. Whereas I think he is always open and welcoming no matter what you've done or been because it is in his nature to be so. He goes in search of the lost sheep, he stands at the door of our lives and knocks – he wants to come in and be with us – he isn't waiting for us to do or be anything, he isn't asking for anything, instead he reaches out with all his heart and offers us his hand in genuine love and friendship. When we see his love for what it really is we will recognise our own shortcomings. It will bring to the fore our sorrow and repentance for where we have failed. Now love is the trigger – and not guilt, which almost always has a negative presence.

Of course, we can refuse to take his hand and turn away but that doesn't mean that the hand of the God of love is ever withdrawn. We can fail to see our shortcomings and where we have failed him, other people and ourselves, but the hand is still held out for us to grasp. He is always ready to come to us and always ready to embrace. The barrier is on our side not on his. This is the image of God which works best for me and it is the one I most readily respond to.

In God's sight we do not fall; in our sight we do not stand. As I see it both of these are true. But the deeper insight belongs to God.[7]
Julian of Norwich

Poor little Jesus
O, poor little Jesus,
This world gonna break your heart,
There'll be no place to lay your head, my Lord.
O, poor little Jesus.
O, Mary the mother,
O, Mary she bow down and cry,
For there's no place to lay his head, my Lord.
O, poor little Jesus.

Come down all you holy angels,
Sing round him with your golden harps,
For some day he will die to save the world.
O, poor little Jesus.

(Traditional USA)
See YouTube: Maddy Prior and The Carnival Band

Bang the drum or shake the hand?

We meet up in Dunoon with another old friend, Jim Macfarlane, who is a retired Church of Scotland minister. Jim has a close working knowledge of the local church scene and is often called on to take services when there is a vacancy in a local parish. He explains that there are too many parishes and too many services. This is because in the eighteenth century a split occurred in the Presbyterian Church in Scotland that pretty much doubled the number of churches overnight. Many of these still need ministers to lead the worship which is why Jim and others are kept busy. The split was partly about patronage and who could appoint ministers and it was partly about the kind of Presbyterianism that was to your liking. The choice was between a church with a strong Biblical literalism as its authority, and something more centre ground known as the Moderate Church with an open approach. The literalists and extremists had to safeguard their purity and a break was made.

This is a very familiar tension in church life. The tension arises out of those different understandings of the death of Jesus mentioned above. Jim tells a story about the recent induction of a minister into a local church where the preacher warned about the judgement to come at the end of time and the gnashing of teeth which is supposed to be part of it, a good example you might say of Biblical literalism. A plaintive voice was heard afterwards putting a spanner in the works because this poor soul didn't have any teeth. The minister said: "Teeth will be supplied".

There is no end to the inventiveness of hardliners. They always have an answer and are not so good at listening. There is an extremism which can take over both politics and religion. We have had too much extremism in recent years. Sometimes it has been violent and horrific, everything from genocide to beheading and terrorism. The hallmarks of extremism include an oversimplification of the issues concerned in usually stark black and white terms; a sometimes adolescent naïvety over causes and outcomes; a belief in absolute solutions that allows little room for co-operation and partnership and a preference for a fight to the death rather than compromise. Neither does extremism have much grasp of a common good that might serve everyone; instead it holds to a total self-belief in its own preferred solutions. We all back our own ideas, whether religious or political, but extremism doesn't want to talk about them in any kind of dialogue or negotiation.

So here's the thing; this is me raising a flag for the virtues of moderation. Why not give being big hearted and open minded a go? Toleration and understanding are underrated. Let's sit down and listen to each other; things will look different if we do because we begin to understand each other and come out from behind our barricades. A common good might be possible that would benefit everyone. Not everything you want can be achieved but some of it might be and this is preferable to denying one side everything it is hoping for. It is often the case in arguments religious and political that the two sides have a good deal in common but they don't like to admit to it.

Loud voices draw most attention. These voices can be heard within the churches and nations of the world. We will always need voices raised for minorities and to lead reform by winning hearts and minds and by righting injustice. But that's not the same as extremism which wants to impose an often minority and factional view. This is why we need to hear more from the centre ground and be spared the destruction that extremism so often inflicts on individuals and communities; and to allow reform to take place when it is needed.

Faith as pilgrimage

Making a journey and being on a pilgrimage scratches below the surface where there is plenty hidden away waiting to be discovered: passing through a Glasgow station you find a story that nobody knew about; look into working life in Glasgow and school life in Edinburgh and you find the influences and circumstances that have been critical in shaping people's lives; ask people to tell the story of how they came to faith and what happened next and the tale they tell is often revealing and surprising; challenge yourself and your faith will be reshaped, better address the life you live and not get stuck in time; challenge extremism and it allows for both the creation of a common good with a wide appeal and timely reform.

Faith and life always have to go together. When faith just won't fit life experience they fall out, have a row. When life won't fit faith we have to ask what's wrong and where change is needed. So, this is me saying no ivory towers of holier than thou belief and no bleak secular urban jungle and no remote rural insularity. Instead, people with faith and heart and soul who walk the pilgrim path but also relish the walk of life.

It is a walk which takes you on a journey that has many twists and turns. You don't know what you will find when you set out. The journey changes you, God is at work. His presence may be hidden – the leaven in the lump, the seed growing secretly, the treasure in the field – because that's how he works in the world he has made which we are part of for a time. Faith is an adventure because we are in a dynamic relationship with God, anything could happen and often does.

Part Two
Sacred Places
Holding hands with the divine

Opposite:
Standing Cross on Skellig St Michael

Four: Holy Loch: protest, sanctuary and dispute

Holy Loch is a name to conjure with. It is a deep-water loch with clear access through the Firth of Clyde to the North Atlantic. The UK submarine divisions were based here during the Second World War and it was here rehearsals were carried out for the invasion of Norway. The Cockleshell Heroes also trained at Holy Loch before their attack on merchant shipping at Bordeaux. The name Holy Loch suggests something sacred but that was to have an increasing irony about it, for some, given the use to which the loch was put as the 1960s got underway.

Holy Loch is not big as lochs go and this is surprising since it was also home to an American submarine base between 1961 and 1992. It was chosen

Holy Loch with St Munn's Church *Daniel Romani*

for its easy Atlantic access when the American military needed somewhere for part of their submarine fleet to refit and for crew turnover. The submarines carried Polaris missiles and were all part of the NATO deterrent. Each Polaris missile carried more destructive power than all the bombs dropped during the Second World War. Once launched they could not be stopped.

Dunoon is the nearest town and provided housing for crew and their families. In return the base provided employment for local people and brought good business, so for all these reasons it was welcomed and became a big presence locally. The submarines and supply ships were permanently on view and became as much part of the landscape as the adjoining woods and rolling hills. But if the locals liked having the Americans living nearby this was not the case for everyone.

The Campaign for Nuclear Disarmament was set on unilateral nuclear disarmament for Britain. Support for this cause always remained small. In 1960 it ran at about 20 per cent amongst the public as a whole. But CND were a significant presence in the political debate of the time and the marches from Aldermaston to London attracted a lot of attention. In Scotland itself there were fears that Scottish culture would be Americanised and the local shipyard business would also take a hit. In addition it was feared that Dunoon and all stations to Glasgow were vulnerable to nuclear attack because of the American presence on Holy Loch.

All this meant that in the early sixties there were protests co-ordinated by a branch of CND known as the Direct Action Committee Against Nuclear War. They protested at Holy Loch, sometimes with a demonstration at the same time in London in Trafalgar Square. They tried to form a barrier with canoes across Holy Loch to stop ships coming and going and an attempt was made to board the *USS Proteus*, the main submarine support vessel. These protests could attract several thousand demonstrators, and reached 12,000 in Trafalgar Square on one occasion. However, they did not manage to dislodge the Americans from Holy Loch and gradually the demonstrations faded.

Bob Reid lived in Dunoon at the time and was brought up there. He was fifteen when the Americans arrived and officers' children attended the local school where Bob was a pupil. He recalls:

We had sit-ins, roadblocks and for many it was their first experience of civil disobedience. The American culture bumped against the more diffident and respectful culture of the West of Scotland. No one had asked the teacher a question until the Americans arrived. They integrated very quickly and made friends of the local population. Some US black kids found it equally odd. I remember a wee guy asking me where his toilet was and being astonished when I said we all went to the same one.

My parents let out our upstairs flat to a black family and we all got on really well introducing each other to our cultures. No doubt we were different but we just ignored that as we had no sophistication or political correctness to get in the way.

My father reluctantly approved of the nuclear base and subscribed to its deterrent value. As a veteran of World War Two he believed it would remove the threat of my brother and I being called up to fight in another war. So far so good!

Visiting Holy Loch today there is nothing to be seen of all the former military activity and protest not to mention the political controversy it caused. The loch is peaceful and picturesque and we "ooh and ah", and mean it, as Bob and Jenny take us on a tour of the area.

St Munn

On the northern bank of the loch is the village of Kilmun and the Church of Scotland parish church of St Munn. This is one of the places which have sparked Bob's interest in retirement. We are pleased to have the advantage of our own bespoke tour guide as Bob takes us round the church. It is officially now redundant as a place of worship and it is being attractively developed as a visitor centre for the area. It is part of an initiative called "Faith in Cowal" (see below and the website of the same name), Cowal being this part of Argyll.

Fintan Munnu was an Irish monk of the seventh century. Ireland is only twelve miles from the Mull of Kintyre and so it is close at hand if you are Irish and wanting to spread your wings. Fintan Munnu was in that frame of mind and decided to come across and travel to Iona on the west coast of Scotland. He hoped to become a monk in St Columba's monastery on the island. But by the time Fintan arrived Columba was dead. The new Abbot turned Fintan down as a member of the community on the grounds, as legend has it, that Columba had predicted that Fintan would arrive and it was Columba's wish that Fintan lead his own monastery. He does exactly this by coming to what is now called Kilmun after Fintan Munnu. Kilmun comes from the Gaelic meaning "the church or cell of St Munnu". Here he established a monastery in about 650. Both Columba and Munnu were key figures in the spread of Celtic Christianity in Scotland and beyond. Because of this and the creation of a monastic community Fintan Munnu was later to be made a saint of the church and so is remembered today as St Munn.

Little now remains of the early occupation by St Munn. The earliest and only artefact of that period was discovered in the adjoining churchyard. It is a carved stone cross of the seventh or eighth century. It may have been a burial memorial stone or perhaps used to symbolically give notice that you were entering a sacred area as you approached the church of that period. From the days of St Munn Kilmun established itself as an important and sacred centre. It was for this reason that by the fifteenth century the loch on which it stands became known as Holy Loch. And it was for this reason that St Munn came to have a close association with the Campbells who were a powerful and ambitious clan. They had moved into Argyll around 1200 and gradually aligned themselves with the monarchy.

The Campbells had fought with Robert the Bruce at Bannockburn when Robert, as King of Scotland, defeated Edward II of England in June 1314 in the First War of Scottish Independence. As a result the Campbells won lands which had been forfeited by rebels who had sided with the English. Duncan was the first Lord Campbell and he cemented his position by marrying Lady Marjorie Stewart, the granddaughter of Robert the Bruce. It was Duncan who established St Munn at Kilmun as the family church and burial place for the heads of the clan who were subsequently Dukes of Argyll. There is a family mausoleum at St Munn's which contains a fine effigy of Duncan and Marjorie. The Dukes of Argyll were all buried here up until 1949. The subsequent Dukes and their families did not appreciate Holy Loch being turned into an American submarine base. It somehow sullied the sacredness of the place and since that time the Dukes and their nearest and dearest have instead been buried at their ancient family home at Loch Awe.

Visitors to St Munn today will see a partly ruined medieval tower to the west of the parish church. It was to this tower that Duncan appointed a Provost and six priests living in community whose task was to pray for the Campbells and so hasten their journey through purgatory. The present church dates from

The stone carved cross at Kilmun dating from the seventh or eighth century. Daniel Romani

the middle of the nineteenth century. It has some good quality stained glass of the period. Its organ is, unusually, powered by a water pump which introduces air to the organ pipes when called on by the organist. It is probably the only water powered organ still in use in Scotland.

It would be difficult to overstate the influence of the monastic communities in bringing faith to the British people. On the back of this the monasteries became both powerful and wealthy. This didn't go down well with Henry VIII. The monasteries were in need of reform but Henry's intervention was much more wide ranging. He thought power and wealth should be in the hands of the monarch alone. He closed down the monasteries in England and helped himself to their wealth.

And it would also be difficult to overstate the predominance of religion in the life of the country at this time. Faith was implicit and it was the political language of the day. Despite this, and often because of it, the country endured the Protestant–Catholic split and the bloodshed that resulted was horrific and heartbreaking. This wasn't a question of one faith against another but one faith at war with itself.

The Cowal Pilgrimage

The "Faith in Cowal" website was started by Dr Gilbert Marcus in 2015 to support a pilgrim route to fifteen pilgrimage sites all with links to Celtic and Medieval Christianity. "Visiting all of these sites will introduce the pilgrim to the whole of Cowal, and to a rich diversity of Scottish Highland landscapes and villages". St Munn is number 10 on the suggested 80-mile

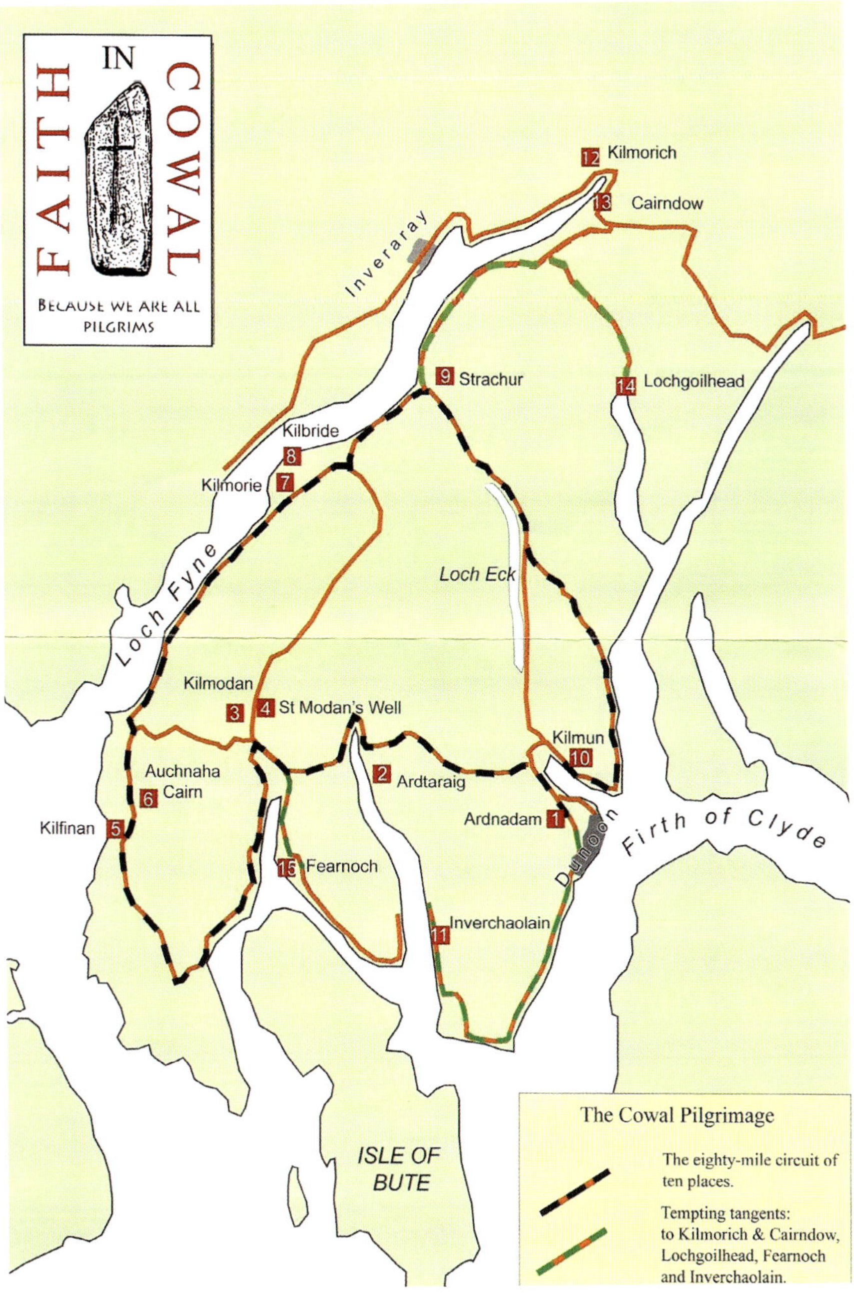
FAITH IN COWAL
BECAUSE WE ARE ALL PILGRIMS
12 Kilmorich
13 Cairndow
Inveraray
9 Strachur
14 Lochgoilhead
Kilbride
8
Kilmorie
7
Loch Fyne
Loch Eck
Kilmodan
3
4 St Modan's Well
Kilmun
10
Auchnaha Cairn
6
2 Ardtaraig
Kilfinan
5
Ardnadam 1
Dunoon
Firth of Clyde
15 Fearnoch
11 Inverchaolain
ISLE OF BUTE
The Cowal Pilgrimage
The eighty-mile circuit of ten places.
Tempting tangents: to Kilmorich & Cairndow, Lochgoilhead, Fearnoch and Inverchaolain.

trail and has the distinction of being the "pilgrim hub" for all of them. It was selected because of its rich historical importance which can be traced from pre-Christian times through the saints Columba and Munnu to the Campbell Clan and the last resting place of the clan chiefs.

The other sites all have their own distinctive features and atmosphere. A "tiny spring of sweet cold water" above St Modan's Well – no. 4 - has been a place of prayer for many centuries. Pilgrims leave pebbles in the water as tokens of the prayers they have said there. Water is also a theme at Kilfinan Church – no. 5 – where a burn "curves around the medieval churchyard" and a symbol of the life-giving water of the pilgrim's faith. The church is the traditional home of the Lamont Clan and memorials to the chiefs of the Clan survive. Kilbride Chapel – no. 7 – commemorates St Brigit who in her day was a popular saint in the Gaelic world. Auchnaha Cairn pre-dates Christianity as a burial place by some two thousand years before Christ. A stone cross of the period suggests a blessing on all those who had gone before, and the faith they held, before the Christian Gospel became known.

The imaginative creation of this pilgrim route has opened up a devotion which introduces travellers to the countryside and landscape of Argyll and also the faith which has had a distinctive influence on the lives of the people who lived there and still do today.

Dispute resolution

If the Christian Faith first came to Argyll through St Munn in the seventh century, some eleven centuries later it was still going strong. A fascinating insight into church and community life there in the early eighteenth century is provided by historical research which Bob Reid has undertaken. He examined the minutes of the Synod of Argyll Visitations conducted in 1701. The record was set down by the clerk to the Presbytery, Duncan McLea. Bob recalls:

Duncan was writing at a time of massive social and economic change. The people of Argyll had endured generations of poverty, famine, vicious local feuds and occupation by Royalist forces. Infant mortality was high. Some children were dying unbaptised due to the lack of ministers.

Religious life had undergone constant change since the Reformation. England had settled on a Protestant monarchy and Scotland was obliged to follow. However, unlike England Scotland favoured Presbyterianism and was under the control of the General Assembly of the Church of Scotland in Edinburgh. Many families who had supported the Stuarts still secretly followed the old Catholic religion or were attracted to the Episcopalian church. Men from some Argyll clans had fought as Jacobites in the Battles of Killiecrankie and Dunkeld in 1689. Some would soon turn out again to support the return of the exiled King James.

Despite pockets of lingering Catholicism, Presbyterianism was well established by 1701 and the Church of Scotland maintained firm control of the Scottish population through a structure of church courts. The General Assembly was the senior controlling body sending its policies and procedures to local synods. They in turn controlled presbyteries who monitored the work of the kirk sessions located in each parish. Argyll had its own synod with presbyteries like Inveraray controlling parishes such as Glenaray.

In 1701 the Synod of Argyll appointed a "Visitatione Committee" to travel to the Parishes of "Kilmaglass" [Strachur], Stralachlan, "Kilfinian" [Kilfinan] and Kilmodan. Their mission was to interrogate ministers, school masters and elders as well as to assess the state of church finances and properties. A key item on every agenda was that of judging parishioners whose conduct was "delinquent".

The Committee was democratically organised and the members elected a chair or Moderator at the start of each session. Although there were Knights and Lairds present it appears that one of the elders was normally elected. Meetings opened with prayer and a bible reading from the local minister. Duncan McLea took the minutes in a businesslike fashion. He included what today would be called "action points" so every decision had a named person responsible and noted for future review.

The Minutes covered meetings at the four parishes and the topics included performance reviews of the minister and school master. Financial audits determined whether local "heretors" [heritors] or landowners were not collecting the Church taxes or "teinds" from tenants or were retaining them. Churches were often in poor states of repair. The Committee spent some time planning repairs. Church bells seemed to regularly go missing.

Where ministers were not being paid or supplied with a manse and glebe the Committee would negotiate some modest financial compensation for the loss. In lieu of a manse Sir Colin Campbell of Ardkinglas supplied Archibald McGillespie, minister at Strachur, with wooden planks to build his own cabin.

On the 15th August 1701 the Committee were sitting at Kilfinan. Their agenda that day included two alleged personal misdemeanours by parishioners. Donald Campbell from "Achichrossan" [Kilfinan] was denying paternity and Henry Lamont, local school master at Kilfinan, was charged with being drunk and neglecting his pupils.

Case 1: Donald Campbell – Kilfinan – 15th August 1701

Donald Campbell had been accused by a local woman, Mary McNeill, of being the father of her child. Duncan had repeatedly denied this. The Moderator pressed him to reply "in the fear of the Lord", whether he was guilty of "fornication" with Mary McNeill and if he was the father of her child. Duncan was not to be intimidated and maintained his previous denials.

The Committee struggled with the case as there was no evidence other than one person's word against another's. As a church court they chose to apply some extra Divine pressure. They decided that he should swear an oath attesting his innocence in front of the entire congregation the next Lord's day. Testifying in front of the congregation would carry enormous significance in an era of regular public naming and shaming. The next stage could have been standing at the Kirk door in sackcloth and "ashenfaced". In case Donald did not share their level of faith he was reminded "of the heinous and tremendous consequences of perjury".

The illustration on the left represents the Committee hearing the case. Duncan is standing at the top of the table gripping his plaid and standing firm. John Campbell the minister of

Kilfinan is offering him several examples of *"God's dreadful and sudden Judgements upon perjorors* [perjurers]".

Duncan McLea is writing the minutes.

Sir Colin Campbell of Ardkinglas is present and Daniel Campbell is the Moderator. The Committee members are rather stumped that the accused is not complying. Mary McNeill was not present.

We do not know if Donald ever repented and admitted his guilt.

Case 2: Henry Lamont – Kilfinan – 15th August 1701

Henry Lamont was the school master for Kilfinan parish. Parents had complained on numerous occasions about his neglecting the pupils through being "given to drinking and company keeping". They wanted him to be discharged and removed. This was also the opinion of the heritors and the elders.

Henry did not deny the charges and after some consideration the "Visitatione Committee" dismissed him and declared his position now vacant. This would have been devastating news for Henry and likely to lead to permanent unemployment and social isolation. However, although the Committee were men of strict religious observance they were not the simply the Taliban in trews. They noted that he had a "numerous family of tender children". They added a merciful note. He was to be paid to the end of the year and then offered the position of "ambulatory" [relief] teacher at a salary of twenty Scots pounds. That is about £2,000 in today's money.

The scene (left) shows Henry standing in front of the elders shuffling his blue bonnet and looking crestfallen. At the table is the clerk Duncan McLea and four elders. The ruling elder, Sir Colin Campbell of Ardkinglas, is absent but his heir James is in attendance.

The author, on the left, with Jenny and Bob Reid

As I read the minutes the characters of the men and their religious commitment leapt from the pages and I realised that religion was not just a key part of Scottish life in the 1700s. It was life itself and all thinking and behaviour was controlled by it. I also learned that the agenda of human life around personal relationships, family, kinship, community and shared beliefs in the 1700s was very similar to the 2000s. It is only our response to them has changed.[8]

Sacred places

The churches of Cowal and Holy Loch are sacred places by association. St Munn was the one who made it so at Kilmun just as St Francis did for Assisi or St Cuthbert at Lindisfarne and St Columba at Iona. The lives of these saints were such that it rubbed off on the places where they lived and called their own.

The White Horse at Uffington was always a special place by association for my mother-in-law, Vera. Her family had come from the nearby village and she had visited there in her childhood. The horse itself is the oldest chalk feature of its kind in Britain and dates from the Bronze Age. Its meaning and purpose are hidden in the mists of time but it may have had a religious significance connected to worship of the sun. It was certainly a special place for Vera because when she died she asked for her ashes to be interred there. It was there she had felt close to her family and close to God and that's where you will find her today.

By contrast I have visited Bec Abbey in Normandy which is also a sacred place because of its atmosphere and with a monastic order of its own. I was captivated by its beauty. The Abbey has had a chequered career. The Abbaye

Notre Dame du Bec Hellouin dates from the eleventh century and is named after a Norman knight called Herlouin who was the driving force behind its foundation. It was from here that Anselm and Llanfranc came to be Archbishops of Canterbury after the Norman Conquest. But the Abbey fell on hard times. Henry V sacked it and the French Revolution turned it into a barracks, with the soldiers' horses stabled in the chapel. It was reinstated as a monastery after 1940 by the French government of the day and there continues to be a small Benedictine Community living and worshipping there today. For me the sacred atmosphere is created by the white stone which was used in the chapel's construction giving a feel of purity and even innocence; by the simplicity of its worship and by the beauty of a life-size statue of the Madonna and Child which stands in the chapel. The statue holds your attention with the motherly charms of a young woman and the vulnerability of the child. But Mary wears a crown and holds a sceptre; this is Mary as the Queen of Heaven according to the Catholic tradition. The statue and the reciting of the monastic offices by the community, when I visited, brought God closer and opened my heart. The silence and beauty of the chapel make it a sacred space to watch and pray.

Madonna and Child, Bec Abbey

Some places by association and others by atmosphere summon up the sacred for those who visit them. It is because in these places a curtain seems to have been drawn back and something that was hidden is revealed. It is here you can see through to another world. It is a world that is beyond this one, in a different dimension to ours. It gives life a meaning which lifts us from just being naked apes to being children of God made in his image and likeness, brothers and sisters to one another. It suggests we are indeed "the stuff that dreams are made on".[9] It puts us in touch with the divine and gives us a hope beyond ourselves. These places are sacred because here we feel we hold hands with God. We have no need to speak or say anything. It is enough to be there with him in the silence and to know that he knows us by name and we are his.

Five: Islands we have loved

Lundy

We have come to the west coast of Scotland to visit the Hebridean island of Islay, more of which later, but first a detour. We like islands and have visited a number around the British coast. In fact, we have the set because we have been to at least one offshore island from the mainland of England, Ireland, Wales and Scotland. In 2018 we went to Lundy Island off the north Devon coast, setting sail from Ilfracombe. When we arrived at Ilfracombe harbour quite a lot of people had already gathered ready to board the MS *Oldenburg*, but there was time for a look around before we were due to depart.

At the time I wrote: *"Hello. Who's this?" The harbour entrance is guarded over by an enormous statue 20 metres tall of a heavily pregnant woman, one arm raised aloft sword in hand, in celebration and defiance. In the other hand she carries the scales of justice and she stands on a set of law books. She's called Verity and is the work of Damien Hirst, who describes this work as a "modern allegory of truth and justice". She was installed in 2012 and is on a twenty-year loan to the town from Hirst himself who lives nearby in Coombe Martin. Verity is cast in bronze and stainless steel and there are cut-away sections to reveal the foetus in the womb. Her stance takes its inspiration from the Little Dancer by Edgar Degas.*

Not all the locals greeted her with open arms but more supported this installation than didn't. She has proved a draw bringing more visitors to the town to see her in all her glory, an impressive sight. The truth and justice theme comes across right enough but there is also something here about women and being a woman. The time was when childbirth was called confinement and women wore loose clothing to cover their bump. Not any longer. Bumps are now often on proud display. Verity is a strong woman, fertile and delighted to be pregnant and don't anyone dare say otherwise, especially men. Women today are in celebration of womanhood, of course. Men have had the say for far too long and often made a mess of it. It has been a long haul but it is time for

Ferry arrival point on Lundy

women to run the world. Our Lady of Ilfracombe says all that and more. We give her a wave as we leave the harbour and head out to Lundy.

There is a party of primary school children on board taking the trip with their teacher and support staff to help with the numbers. The teacher is young and attentive and clearly enjoys the children and being with them. They have no doubt done preparation work with her in class and now the great day has come to make the trip. Teachers have the responsibility for thirty children every day of the week and she takes this sea adventure in her stride. I could have done it when I was her age but now my old friend anxiety would be sniffing around and causing trouble. I would be too overtaken with worry about something going wrong and one of the kids going overboard or getting lost. Getting old is all right but it's certainly different from the energy and enthusiasm of the early years and it can take advantage of you when you least expect it. Be off, you anxious troublemaker, before I take the strap to you.

I get talking to the Chair of Governors. I was a Chair of Governors and so know that world of interaction between governors and school. It used to mean little more than being a benign presence on sports day. The Governors meetings were short.

The Chair before me said that when she started there were three items on the agenda and one of those was the date of the next meeting. Then the Government dropped Local Management of Schools onto governing bodies from a great height and with not so much as a by your leave. Governors' meetings can now last long into the evening as they plough through everything from the drains to HR.

This Chair of Governors knows all about that but he is still there and today making the Lundy trip as well in good humour and with evident enjoyment. He is testimony to the many people around the country who out of generosity and kindness support others – schools and hospitals and care homes included – and do it for love. We live in a "me me" culture, or so we are told, and in some ways we do. But there are also many people who give their time and talents gladly to their local community and gain great satisfaction in doing so. This Chair of Governors is one of them but doesn't make great show of it because he is modest and unassuming and just glad to be on board in every sense of the word. TV and films and the media often show us images of the world gone wrong. It can have a corrosive effect. They are right to do so, because there are things we don't like but need to face up to, but it's not the whole story. There is also genuine goodness and kindness in abundance, often from ordinary people who have them firmly in their hearts.

All this takes place on deck but we have found some seats inside and settle down for the two-hour trip. There is another party on this journey, mostly at the other end of the age spectrum from the primary school. They are identifiable by their name badges. The two opposite us chat a bit but they are much consumed reading every column inch in today's Daily Telegraph. This is not an easy task in a confined space. The Telegraph is a broadsheet and hasn't given way to the smaller, more ready to hand, tabloid format. One way to read it is to hold the whole paper out in front with arms outstretched, as though you are about to greet a long-lost family member. This works for a time but arms soon become tired. An alternative is to lay it flat on the table in front of you, carefully avoiding encroaching on the space of the people opposite (that's us) and shuffling through the pages one by one, but there's not a lot of room on a small table to do this. You can also fold so just the bit you are presently grappling with is visible to the naked eye. The result is that what started out as a neatly presented paper which Queen Victoria would have been proud of (she liked her daily paper ironed before she read it) soon becomes something best given over to the recycling. In addition if there are two of you and you are sharing you have to decide or barter about who gets which pages first. Married couples will not find this necessarily enhances their relationship.

Unlike the school children we haven't done much by way of preparation for this visit. When we arrive at Lundy we are surprised to find that the first challenge is a climb up from the modest harbour to the plateau which is the main part of the island. Blimey it's steep! I have to make regular stops to recover before pressing on. At the top rough moorland with heather and gorse stretches along the coast. We take the coastal path looking out to sea as we go. It is a beautiful sunny day and we enjoy the air and the view for their own sake.

One of the draws of Lundy is the birdwatching but sadly no birds of note are coming our way. Their favoured habitat, we read on our leaflet about the island, is too far along the coast for us to be able to make it in the time available or perhaps we, and mostly me, are too feeble to set a sufficient pace to get there. All that uphill bit to get this far has taken its toll.

A few people live on the island and there is a pub and shop which seem to be at the heart of community life. There is also a church which was built in the nineteenth century by the Revd Hudson Heaven so that Lundy became known, wouldn't you know it, as the Kingdom of Heaven. I can see you really need to come and stay to get a proper feel for the place and love it, which clearly many do. There are plenty of places where you can do this including the now adapted castle built by Henry III in 1244. The castle was paid for by the sale of rabbits because Lundy was a royal warren at the time. It was the pirates of the day Henry was worried about, who, amongst other things, poached his rabbits. The castle was built to keep them in their place, rabbits and pirates. "Yo ho ho, it's rabbit pie for me" but not if you get caught by the King's men at the castle, "Come here, my lad, no more rabbit pie for you".

Skomer

The first visit we made to an offshore island was Skomer, off the Pembrokeshire coast in southwest Wales. That was in the 1970s and we have returned many times since. A boat runs from St Martin's Haven and when we started going you phoned up the skipper, or more probably the skipper's wife , the night before to see if he was going to go the next day; it all depended on the weather. Now you can look on line, of course, and now you have to get there really early to be sure of getting on the boat and getting onto the island at all. Numbers permitted to land are limited to 250 each day.

Landing may have improved now, it's a while since we have been, but early on it was not a gentle glide along a pier and all safely tied up before you step ashore as it is with Lundy. Back then you had to judge the swell and as the boat rose and fell step off at a good moment on to what was a craggy rock face before ascending on to firmer ground. Ginny did it once when she was seven months pregnant and survived to tell the tale.

All this is because Skomer is one of those magical places that has been preserved not for our sakes but for the sake of the birds that live and breed there. These include razorbills and guillemots and everyone's favourite the puffin. Puffins aren't there all the year but in May and June they can be readily seen before going back out to sea.

They come to breed and use the abandoned rabbit holes for nesting. They have no fear of humans so scrabble around your feet but fiercely defend their nests if you get too close. The razorbills and guillemots rise and soar on the air currents along the cliff faces and at night Manx shearwaters return to the island with their eerie call penetrating in the darkness.

Place matters and everyone needs special places they know and love and can hold in their hearts. When you can't actually make it there, or, on cold winter nights when you are sat by the fire, you can go there in your imagination and remember earlier trips and adventures. For us Skomer holds all those days of early married life and just setting out. We don't slosh about too much in nostalgia but these memories are like family treasures or old friends. It's just nice to have them by you and meet up from time to time and give a little cheer for having been there and been together. It is transcendence because it takes you out of yourself and puts you in touch with something bigger and better. It speaks of life as being more than the

pragmatic and difficult and reminds you that there is always light and hope from above to be found in nature all around you.

In his best selling book *English Pastoral* James Rebanks paints a picture of modern farming in Britain. He is himself a farmer in Cumbria. He is critical of what he calls industrial farming or the intensive post-war model of farming. He thinks that soil fertility and sustainability as well as wildlife have been put at risk by too much dependence on chemicals to keep the soil fertile and eliminate pests and disease. Many have said the same but his voice is authentic because he speaks from within the farming community he knows well.[9a]

The government has now linked good environmentally friendly farming practise to government subsidies for farmers. The hope is that this will counter the destruction which some practises have clearly brought to wildlife and the environment in general.

Skomer is a place where bird life is protected and species thrive. What is needed is for wildlife preservation and nurture to be given the same priority everywhere and in all we do. We too easily lose sight of being stewards of nature charged with caring for the environment so that it can be sustained and renewed and preserved. Too much has already been lost. Skomer stands out as a beacon of good practise.

The Skelligs

The top prize in our book for an island that offers a window into the transcendent are the Skelligs off the southwest coast of Ireland. We discovered these by accident in days before the whole world had come to camp at their door. In recent years they have been used as a film set (for *Star Wars*) and sometimes with disastrous results. In 2014 black-legged kittiwake chicks in their nests were apparently swept into the sea by the downdraught of a helicopter and devoured by predatory gulls.

You access the Skelligs from Port Magee, where we had landed up one summer as we explored Ireland's west coast. We found a very comfortable B and B and settled in. Port Magee is opposite Valencia Island. It was from here that the first successful transatlantic cable was laid in the 1860s. The next day we went to Catholic Mass there. Happily there was no one on the door to check we are fully signed up Catholics and of the true faith, so a couple of oddball Anglicans mix in nicely with perhaps 250 locals of all ages. In the Catholic tradition it seems the great thing is to be there, it's attendance that matters rather than what goes on once you are in your pew or, as with some of the men, skulking outside but there none the less. The priest gets the whole thing done in 45 minutes or less and our landlady said he's rather slow.

"I won't be keeping you."

"Oh thank you, Father, look after yourself now."

You go to Ireland for three things apart from the Mass: the craic, the music and the Guinness. All three are served up in every good pub in Ireland and The Moorings at Port Magee is no exception. The Guinness tastes different in Ireland, the music has a mind of its own and the craic never comes to an end, there is always another story to tell. The great thing about traditional Irish music is that it keeps going and going, especially the jigs. You would think it might be boring after a time as the fiddle goes round again but it isn't; every limb is moving, every heart is singing. Jigs give you energy and enthusiasm for life. They're a bit like a strong cup of coffee without all that caffeine swilling round your bloodstream.

It was always the case, at the time he wrote them, that Shakespeare's plays ended with the cast performing a jig on stage, the audience clapping and cheering, and they still do at The Globe. The actors have said it, the audience has heard it. The writer has put into words what we think and believe and

Little Skellig with Skellig St Michael behind *Ginny Eaton*

hope for – Yes! That's it; that's what I think matters more than anything else. So let's break out in dancing in celebration of the richness of life and all that it brings; nothing else says it in the same way as dancing a jig with energy and commitment.

In the film *Shakespeare in Love* the writer Tom Stoppard recreated the first performance of *Romeo and Juliet*. At the end there is complete silence. The actors think they've bombed. Then from nowhere comes a great roar and a cheer. Our Will has said it all and said it well: Love is what binds our hearts together, love is all and love is everything. What else would we do but dance a jig and dance the night away.

So after a great night at The Moorings we are up and down the quay the next morning to get the boat to the Skelligs. £25 each then, rather more now, I imagine. We have to wait for the diesel to be delivered, this is Ireland after all, but at 10.50 we set sail. There are fourteen of us on board plus the skipper and his mate. The weather is fine after a drizzly start. We roll and pitch a bit but are OK, we like to think, because of the homeopathic travel pills we took earlier. An hour and a half gets us to the first of the Skelligs, Little Skellig.

The Skelligs lie some eight miles off the southwest tip of southern Ireland, out from the Iveragh Peninsula in County Kerry. There are two of them, Little Skellig and Skellig St Michael. Little Skellig is closed to the public and home to nearly 30,000 pairs of northern gannets. They nest on the sheer rock face and have turned the island white with their droppings. Little Skellig is about one mile in length and reaches 134 metres into the Atlantic air.

The gannets fish in the sea around the island and further afield. They can be seen waiting and ready in the sky above and looking with piercing eyesight into the waters beneath. Then, when they think the time has come they dive – with wings closed behind them and, they hope, pinpoint accuracy – like a high-powered rocket, into the sea. How often they are successful in catching a fish supper is hard to say; maybe you just keep going until a plump cod or haddock is yours and with one gulp dinner is over and you can return to shore, or rock in this case, to feed your chicks who wait eagerly with opened beak for your return and regurgitation.

The other Skellig is Skellig St Michael. It's here you can land but to do so you have to adopt the same approach as you do for Skomer. Ride with the swell and take a leap of faith when land and boat are in alignment. We make it and begin to make the ascent. Skellig St Michael is a World Heritage Site because here in the sixth century monks came from mainland Europe and settled in a monastery they made themselves with beehive-like constructions from stones available on the island. The monastery where they lived, ate and worshipped is still there and pretty much as they left it. It's 600 steps to reach their airy heavenly dwelling and fortunately there are some flat bits which make for a breather as you go. It is a unique experience to share their world for a short while. It is not a big site. It gives a tremendous view of the mainland to which the monks must have rowed for the essentials this rocky outcrop couldn't supply. They were on a mission. Like St Columba they took with them faith to share with those they met when they travelled. Skellig St Michael was for them a safe haven to return to and their touchstone with God. Here they could breathe him in deeply and distil his presence from the silence and the crashing of the waves and the screeching of the gannets.

It is the atmosphere and the glory of the place which sets it apart. It is this which puts you in touch with the divine. Words have their place but the deeper things of life, and heaven, are often beyond words and it is those we find here. It is fourteen hundred years since it got going. Old doesn't necessarily mean better but the past has a few tales to tell and many things are the same now as they were then. The need to reach out beyond ourselves is one of them and to know you have touched something which is not of this world but real and true and sacred.

The gospel story is exactly that. The life and death of Jesus resonates in our lives and the strongest images it gives us are those that are most human: the Cross, the Madonna and Child where Mary holds the baby Jesus, the Pietà as Mary holds in her arms Jesus taken down from the Cross. We come to God through *our* humanity; he comes to us through *his* humanity. It's this which inspired those sixth-century monks and why they stayed and it became a sacred place. It's why we visited and couldn't believe our eyes when we did.

David Scott is a priest poet and a friend. He has won national awards for his poetry and is recognised today as a leading Christian poet. He too visited the Skelligs and wrote this poem as a result.

Skellig St Michael: A Pilgrimage
I was on top of an illuminated wave
The ones you don't believe when you
See them in manuscripts, an upturned "U",
or on top of a Leviathan, but it was true.
The boat climbed the wave, sat on
top of it, and slid down the other side.
We had the childhood colours too:
Blue boat, black sea, white faces.

On arrival the sea doesn't give you up,
but still rolls, and even in your dreams
you will be surging and plummeting,
or leaping off the cliffs like a puffin
which takes a leisurely fifty feet to ease
out of its fall, and tucks its orange feet
behind, and squits its white stuff
like parachutes on to the rocks.

It's only when you leave the lighthouse path
strewn with the skeletons of birds
and thick with a high-pitched smell of bird lime
that you begin to hear the silence
pressing in, far from the engine of the boat
and the orchestrated scream of gulls.

Then the steps begin, the Southern Stairway,
counting six hundred up to an unknown bedroom.
Somehow it felt necessary to be discalced,
my feet, white as a gannet's breast, my boots
hanging round my neck like earrings.
The boatman I noticed, stayed below.

Rightly, to enter the enclosure you have
to stoop, awkwardly, lowly. You begin by bowing.
In, you cannot see your way out.
The first miracle will be if you are alone,
the second that the sun will shine, the third

"Six hundred (steps) to an unknown bedroom."

"To enter... you begin by bowing."

that God will talk with you. Pray to St Michael
for three miracles, whose skellig it is. Stop.
Breathe. Let in the peace, and if you don't kneel there
where on earth will you kneel?

I looked up and saw an angel standing by the tombs.
She was dressed in brown. She was the guide,
She understood the need for silence.

We can know too much.

This is where the guide books stop and the poems begin.
This is where we have to imagine the monks
watching the sky with nothing
between themselves and heaven,
a psalter for food, rain for drink, and possibly
a strip of wheat beyond the enclosure.
This desert is on the edge of the ocean
and they made the edge a virtue.

But surely despair was sometimes the shape
of their beehive hut, a homesickness, when
the elements took leave of God's control
and became something other. Surely, for some,
having said goodbye to the world,
death could not come quickly enough.

A part of us will not come down:
the glimpse of heroism we could never really manage,
a crazy love of Christ, a romance, something
to do with penitence. And as we sit in meetings
In our suits, we'll take the boat again, and climb
with the gulls willing us up further into the lightness
for which prayer is the only music, and Christ's coming
the only purpose under heaven.[10]

Six: Islay is magic

Persabus

The big reason we have made this trip is to go to the Inner Hebridean island of Islay – pronounced, we discover, "eye-la". We take our leave of Jenny and Bob, who drive us to Inveraray to catch the bus for the next stage of the journey. Jen also prepares sandwiches for us to take with us.

"Thanks, Jen, you're a saint."

"Oh yes, that's me; move over, Mother Teresa."

Inveraray is the seat of the Dukes of Argyll and was established as a town in 1745 by the Third Duke. As part of Bob's conducted tour we had had a glimpse of the Third Duke at St Munn's church on Holy Loch, which is where the family mausoleum can be found and he is safely laid to rest. Rest in peace: you did a good job here. Inveraray has a commanding position overlooking Loch Fyne and is a set piece of Scottish Georgian architecture. Key buildings to take a closer look at are the neo-classical church, and the Jail and Court House, now happily an award-winning museum. Inveraray Castle is occupied by the current Duke and his family. Visitors are welcome. But no time for all this today – only a quick coffee and a fond goodbye to Bob and Jenny as we board the coach which arrives on time from Glasgow.

The coach is bound for Campbeltown at the far end of Kintyre, having driven down the coast road through Argyll. It is here that you find the Mull of Kintyre and memories of Paul McCartney's 1977 hit come flooding back.

The video has the Pipe Band of Campbeltown processing on the beach with kilts swinging and the pipes filling the air. It's a Wings' number and Linda is there and what looks like their family cottage in the background on the shoreline of the Mull of Kintyre itself.

In a dusty cupboard I have a November 1969 copy of *Life* Magazine, don't ask, which featured Paul and Linda and two of their, then kids, Heather and Mary, on the front cover. There had been a rumour that Paul had gone missing and might even be dead. It was all nonsense of course and here was photographic evidence that he was still very much alive and well and in Scotland. The headline is *Paul is still with us*. The photograph looks as though it was taken on the Mull of Kintyre and this is where they were living at the time, glad to be out of the public gaze, I imagine.

Paul comes across as someone who has a lot of Scouse zest for life and living but it is not hard to see what a huge loss Linda's premature death must have been to him and their family. It is said he wept every day for a year. If true it shows how deep the river of true love runs and how much loss affects those left behind. It is easy to underestimate grief and its impact. Sadly Paul came to know only too well what it means. Linda died of breast cancer; she was 56.

We are not going as far as Campbeltown or the Mull of Kintyre but get off at Kennacraig, which is the ferry terminal for the boat going to Islay. She's called *Finlaggan* and we discover why later when we begin to explore the island. Like all the island ferries she is run by Caledonian MacBrayne. There is plenty of room and we find good seats by a window. There is a café for drinks and eats. Passengers are already tucking in. You can also go outside onto an open deck which looks aft as we steam away from Kennacraig and make passage towards Port Askaig on Islay.

I am always a bit wary of sea trips ever since an unforgettable Channel crossing in one of those fast catamarans. Fast they may be but low in the water they are as well and so we picked up every slight turbulence on the way. The Captain came across the PA with "We are now leaving the safety of Boulogne harbour" and the catamaran went nearly vertical. I was not alone in clasping a black plastic bag close to my person for the rest of the trip.

Thankfully the *Finlaggan* is a lot more substantial, a proper ferry as you might say, and the sea is calm. We make good and smooth progress for the two hours the crossing takes.

The Happy Farmer drives Old Lizzie, a favourite classic from the world of tractors

On arrival we pick up a hire car and head for Persabus Farm where we are to stay. Persabus is run by Donald and Rosemary Fletcher. It's a shared venture but Donald seems to mostly do the farming and Rosemary sees to the guests as well as running a small café and pottery in a farm outbuilding. They are warm and welcoming and we settle in to one of their comfortable self-catering cottages adjacent to the farmhouse.

Rosemary is a blogger and Donald often features in the blog:

Last night Donald went visiting the guests in the cottages armed with homemade clootie dumpling and a bottle of whisky, needless to say what set out as a ten minute quick "hello" saw him not returning until the small wee hours... a good time was had by all.

Donald is also known as The Happy Farmer. His family have been farming on Islay for many generations and in this blog Rosemary recalls a lucky find arising from road-building excavations a few years ago.

Outside the pottery stands the old priest stone. Once used for baptisms and blessings it was also rescued by my late father-in-law in the 1970s. A company from the mainland were on the island building a new main road, the spoil and rubble was being tipped on Persabus. The Happy Farmer's father had heard from his forefathers of an old priest stone that had long gone missing and was thought to be buried in the land being dug out by the contractors. My father-in-law went raking through the tonnes of rubble. Against the odds, in among hundreds of tonnes of waste, he found a large stone and with his pocketknife clearing the mud, he discovered the 'cup' of the stone. He had found the priest stone. He always maintained this special stone saved itself and that he was led to it. Without heavy lifting gear the stone had to be dragged from the rubble heap by rope all the way from Caolila to Persabus. The white mark lay engraved in the road for many years and the priest stone was saved for generations to come.

It is fitting that 'the old boy' as he is affectionately remembered found the priest stone. Persabus gets its name from the Norse invasions, Persa meaning priest and bus meaning abode. Persabus translates to home of the priest and now has its priest's stone back.[11]

Sheep may safely graze on Islay.

St Columba's

The next day is Sunday so we head off for the island's Scottish Episcopal Church of St Columba which is at Bridgend just off the A826, the main road which runs across the island. This isn't, of course, Presbyterian and Church of Scotland, but part of the Scottish Episcopal Church and the Anglican Communion, which gives it a eucharistic preference. Here this doesn't mean smells and bells as in some places but a simple communion service. Vestments are worn by the priest. For us, good middle of the road Anglicans that we are, it is all very familiar territory and we feel at home.

The church itself is rectangular in design rather than cruciform. It is nineteenth century with white to cream painted wood panel walls inside. The windows are framed in iron and made up of small three- or four-inch squares glazed in varied light colours. Over the years some of these have

The High Cross of Kildalton *Shutterstock*

broken and been replaced with clear glass. Together they let in the light which on a sunny day, like today, floods all around and lifts the spirit. Four or five wooden pews range down each side of the building in the usual way. There is no defined, narrowed down chancel leading to a sanctuary but there is a simple choir with stalls, and an altar on the east wall. This has not been brought forward, as in many churches today, so the priest can stand behind. I learn afterwards that this is because it is made of marble and not practical to move. Here the priest faces east when celebrating instead, back to the congregation, and in the traditional manner. The altar is dressed in green for the Trinity season and a spare altar frontal in red has been placed above the altar to act as a reredos. "Sanctus, Sanctus, Sanctus" is embroidered across the top in large letters. All this works surprisingly well. On the altar a burse and veil cover the chalice and paten, placed centrally and also dressed in matching green for the season. Candles are in place.

We are greeted on arrival and I am glad to say not profusely but not indifferently either: a smile and a nod which is just right. Handed the books for the service we sit down to collect our thoughts. We are nine in all including the priest. The candles have been forgotten, so when the priest comes in to begin the organist hurries forward, white hair flowing behind and in white open-neck shirt, to light them. He has a cigarette lighter in hand to do this but the lighter doesn't understand what it's supposed to do and he struggles to keep a flame alive on the candle. We all watch intently, willing him on. Once he does keep one going he lights one candle from the other rather than risk wrestling with lighter and candle for a second time. Ah! that's got it. He retires to the safety of the organ stall for the rest of the service.

The priest has waited patiently while all this takes place but is now able to announce the first hymn: William Cowper's "Through all the changing scenes of Life". The hymn book is *Ancient and Modern Revised*, dating from the forties or fifties, so it has all the traditional Anglican hymns in abundance, of which this is one. It is one of William Cowper's Olney hymns which he wrote alongside those of the converted slave trader John Newton. They lived together in Olney in Buckinghamshire.

Cowper insisted that his name was not pronounced Cooper – as some would have it, wanting to spare him any unfortunate farmyard associations – but Cowper, as it is spelt. He was a sensitive soul and suffered from depression and mental ill health. It was in recognition of this that David Cecil called his biography of Cowper *The Stricken Deer*. I have always felt an empathy with William. This opening hymn at today's service captures something of his struggle. I think John Newton must have been a confident, larger than life character, which as a slave trader you would have to have been. Someone of William's disposition would have found shelter from the storm under his wing, a hand to hold, as well as a faith to share. To his credit Newton later apologised for his part in the slave trade and became an abolitionist. His change of heart was brought about by his conversion to the Christian Faith. In 1788 he published *Thoughts upon the African Slave Trade*, in which he described what he had witnessed as captain of a slave ship. He was later ordained and became parish priest at Olney. He was also a hymn writer, his most famous hymn being "Amazing Grace", which expresses perhaps his own sense of gratitude and wonder at the grace of God, summed up also in William Cowper's hymn we sing this morning:

Through all the changing scenes of life,
In trouble and in joy;
the praises of my God shall still,
my heart and tongue employ.
…
When in distress to him I called
he to my rescue came.

We sing out and look up as we do so at the east window. There is no stained glass but an image of a large Celtic Cross has been impressed on the clear glass underneath. This is a local treasure, the High Cross of Kildalton. It was cut from one piece of local stone and is widely regarded as a masterpiece of early Christian carving dating from the ninth century. The same image is also woven into the carpet that leads up to the altar.

The service is a 1970s re-ordering of the Scottish Liturgy of the Communion Service from the Scottish Prayer Book. The original service was drawn up in 1637. Many of the phrases and much of the wording are familiar from the Book of Common Prayer used south of the border. The priest, whose name we learn afterwards is Keith Pagan, was the parish priest here before retiring to Campbeltown. He is now in his eighties. He is one of a small band of priests I have known whose names resonate with their calling – Paradise and Heaven (of Kingdom of Heaven fame) being some of the others. They must all their lives have had the trial of fielding comments: "I've heard all the jokes", as my friend Bryan Paradise used to say. Bishops have the same problem. A former Bishop of Guildford told a story of a woman who in astonishment at what she thought was a coincidence said to him, "Fancy your name being Guildford!" It's all part of the mystery of church life that Bishops sign themselves with the name of their diocese. Not everyone knows this.

They only have one service a month at St Columba's. It's on the third Sunday and there is some difficulty in finding a priest to preside. Keith seems happy enough to be here and is just what you want in a priest, he's modest and unassuming. He does the liturgy but does not intrude so there is a sense of reverence which conveys a feeling of contentment in me and in him.

The Gospel for the day is the Lost Sheep and the Lost Coin. Keith says that the Pharisees put your failures and the need to confess before their

The men of the kirk deciding on the split after much thought and prayer (From a contemporary engraving).

acceptance of you – grovel and we'll talk to you. But Jesus has it the other way round. He accepted, without reserve, the people who came to him and went out looking for those who were lost. After that he was happy to talk about what might be amiss and need correction, but not before, because he welcomed the people he met with open arms. This was especially true for those who were down on their luck, poor, sick and in greatest need. That is gospel for me and I give a cheer for a good sermon nicely delivered.

We talk afterwards and I tell Keith I am a retired priest too. The church has accommodation for locum clergy and is happy to receive visiting priests and can put them up. I might give it a go.

St Columba's is not the only church on the island. We also visit the Round Church which stands in the middle of Bowmore, the administrative capital and shopping centre for Islay. Bowmore is situated on Loch Indaal and is the home of the Bowmore Distillery. The Round Church is the parish church of Kilarrow and was built in 1767 by the Laird of Islay at the time, Daniel

Campbell. He also planned and built the village of Bowmore with the church at the top of a wide and central street. The church stands out as a distinctive feature and has a tower looking uncannily like a lighthouse. The church is round, the story goes, so that there are no corners for the devil to hide in. Inside a large print is displayed which shows the good and the great of the mid-eighteenth century, all men of course, signing up to go their separate ways when the Presbyterian churches split.

Perhaps the devil didn't worry too much about not being able to hide in the corners; a church that was breaking up and falling apart was a good day's work he could be pleased with.

A wee dram to blow your head off

Islay is famous for its whisky and it draws many visitors each year to its ten distilleries. Whisky, as every whisky buff knows, can be divided into different types. There are blended whiskies (yuk!), there are whiskies made from grain (mostly wheat), and then there are single malt whiskies made from barley. "Single" means coming from only one distillery. The single malts are the queens of whisky production and the true connoisseurs are not interested in anything else. It is why they come to Islay which specialises in these: to see how they are produced and to sample them for themselves.

All single malt whiskies are made in the same way with the same three essential ingredients which are malted barley + yeast + water but these ingredients vary from place to place. These locally sourced ingredients all bring their own distinctive flavour to the final product. On Islay, for example, this means that the whisky ends up with a smoky flavour, by contrast to Speyside where the end result is sweeter. Peat is also involved although, as we shall see, not as an ingredient. Whisky is produced around the world but there is nothing like Scottish whisky which is renowned as the granddaddy of them all.

All the distilleries on the island offer guided tours which traditionally end with a tasting and the chance to buy a bottle or three – at a price. The best doesn't come cheap. The tours differ in length depending on whether you're a connoisseur looking for an in-depth nose round and a chance to air what you know or, like us, passing tourists just taking an interest. We opt for the short one-hour tour and choose the Bunnahabhain Distillery (pronounced "Bunna-have-in", for the uninitiated like us). It's just up the road from Persabus Farm where we are staying.

We are a small party of a dozen or so and a member of the distillery team gives an excellent introduction to whisky production as she takes us round. Bunnahabhain has struggled recently but has now received investment from overseas and there is evidence of a new visitor centre being built. My guidebook tells me that this distillery is "really only for the obsessives" and

Stills used for large-scale whisky production.

only in production for a few months each year. But with the new dosh and better visitor facilities coming on board it looks as though this is about to change. The distillery tours seem to be quite big business and upgrading should mean many more than the obsessives will be coming to see how it's done here. The whisky-making process is the same wherever it is carried out, as we learn from our tour guide, and some background reading. The barley is taken, soaked in local spring water and allowed to germinate for eight to ten days. It is then dried out in large peat-fired vats which use local peat, giving that distinctive Islay flavour. This process is known as malting. We peer into huge vats which seem to boil and bubble, pass large copper vessels, abstain from flash photography, as we are told, and nod at the very few attendants who oversee all this process. Whisky-making doesn't seem to be labour intensive but is nevertheless an important source of local employment.

The malt is then ground into a "grist", hot water added and drained and yeast also added, creating a sweet liquid called "wort". After this various distillations take place and, believe it or not, gunpowder is used and lit to test whether the emerging whisky is ready, or not. This is all part of the whisky maker's dark art that surrounds the entire production process. Finally, the liquid is matured in oak casks for at least three years. These casks are bought in from sherry and wine producers and the left-behind flavour from this former use gives the whisky yet another element and so creating its own distinctive character.

The tour ends and we retire to the shop for our wee dram. Unfortunately I am not listening carefully enough, as usual, and don't pick up that the sample we have chosen is usually taken with a liberal addition of water and only sipped rather than slugged back, as you would expect any virile male worth the name would do. So slug it back I go and nearly fall over. It is a blow your head off moment and my head seems to have been scattered around the shop. I stagger outside. Nurse Ginny brings water to dowse the flames and after a good deal of coughing and expletives I recover enough to go back inside. Part of the problem was that this particular malt is over 60 per cent proof and so I have been consuming near neat alcohol, which at my time of life and being virtually teetotal is probably not a sensible thing to do, as the A and E nurse isn't slow in pointing out. As she explains I have no one to blame but myself, which is true.

Where eagles dare

The RSPB have two reserves on Islay. One in the north centred on Loch Gruinart and one in the southwest corner on the Oa – pronounced "O". Each Tuesday, we learn from the Information Centre, a RSPB guide leads a conducted walk of about two miles, so we decide to give it a go.

The car park near the coast is the assembly point and when we arrive about twenty others are already there. The guide is a young lady called Shona-Isla, appropriately, who is collecting the money and getting things organised. She has a telescope for bird spotting which she carries in a frame on her back. We set off but have not been going long when she calls a halt and points over to the coast. With binoculars we locate some choughs bouncing and swooping along, as they do, above the cliff edge.

We know about choughs because, although they are rare, we have seen them in southwest Wales and Cornwall. They are members of the crow family just under 40 cm in length. Their distinguishing and distinguished feature are their red legs and curved red beak. Show us your legs, we say. We can't pick these up as we are too far distant but it is still good to see some old friends again. Shona-Isla says there are three families on the Oa Reserve and about 45 pairs on Islay as a whole. The RSPB are encouraging them to stay and so keeping our distance is part of not disturbing them and letting them breed and become established. We learn a small breeding pool makes it difficult for them to reproduce. So, having given them the full birdwatching experience with telescope, binoculars and naked eye, we let them get on with it and we move on.

We are mostly retired in the group but there is one young family and mum carries a young baby girl on her front in a baby carrier. It looks as though this baby has two mums because her parents are a gay couple and we chat to them as we go along. Baby snuggles in and enjoys the love and comfort of being carried close to mum and like the choughs bounces along as we go.

We pass a herd of Highland cattle. They give us the once over as we go by, with that eyeball to eyeball stare that only cattle know how to turn on. They are not what you would call chatty and keep chewing the grass and the cud as we wind our way through them. They are the tight-lipped locals casting a suspicious eye over visitors and keeping their thoughts to themselves as they do so. Part of the reason for their being here is an RSPB strategy to encourage bird life. The cattle and sheep chew the grass and expose the grubs and insects the birds feed on. This is particularly the case for the choughs and a strategy adopted successfully in Cornwall too. The choughs can't get to the food they need without it. Biodiversity is a wonderful thing and more complicated than you might think. This is exactly the point of course and why cattle and sheep play a key part if bird life is to flourish.

Next it's the eagles. We pause on a headland and look over to another across a small inlet. And sure enough this is where eagles dare. Shona-Isla points out these birds of prey soaring above. As with the choughs we are at a distance here and the eagles appear as black outlines on the horizon, but eagles they are. There are only two pairs on the Oa Reserve with around nine pairs on Islay altogether. The two Oa families are out this morning for a bit of exercise before an early lunch. One pair have their fledgling with them and the three swoop and dive together. We watch keenly and point out

Shona-Isla with her telescope.

to one another where they have all now got to.

"Just there, see, above that sticking up bit and to the left."

"Ah yes, got it."

Seeing so many is a lucky find and Shona-Isla can't quite believe our luck, or hers. She has done a good job showing us where to go and where to look. We loiter with intent for some time. Eagles have a wingspan of about 2 metres and deserve all of the reputation they have for being magnificent and awe inspiring so that even at a distance we pick this up. It's a bit like seeing royalty and something to tell our grandchildren when we get back.

After some time eagle watching we walk on and follow the track to the American Monument which stands above the Mull of Oa. More than the birdwatching this is the main reason people come to the Oa, evidenced by the duck boarding which has been laid to the Monument along the direct route from the car park. It is a biggy, this monument, and shaped like a lighthouse but with no lamp. When it comes to monuments Americans don't do things by half. It was erected by the American National Red Cross in memory of those who died in two naval disasters in 1918.

The first disaster happened in February 1918 when the American troop ship SS *Tuscania*, carrying over two thousand American army personnel, was torpedoed by a German U-Boat seven miles offshore. When the lifeboats were lowered the ropes broke and many of the soldiers were thrown into the sea; 266 were drowned. The Monument also commemorates the loss of life when HMS *Otranto* was shipwrecked in the nearby waters off Kilchoman in October 1918.

The inscription on the Monument reads:

On Fame's eternal camping ground, their silent tents are spread, while glory keeps with solemn round, the bivouac of the dead.

I can't quite picture what this metaphor is describing but the intention is clear as is the tragedy and loss of both these disasters. We pause and think how bad it must have been for those on board both ships and what they went through together at the time. Disasters like these, especially when related to wartime, attract a lot of attention. When I first was ordained it looked as though Remembrance Sunday would die out as less and less people could remember or were actually themselves caught up in war. In fact the reverse has happened. In a time when faith, and Christian faith in particular, has lost ground in the west these great disasters and wartime events seem to act like a religious touchstone. They fill the hole in our lives which the absence of formal religion has left. There is here something serious and ultimate that can't be avoided, that brings us up short and that we must all face at some time. Happy consumerism isn't enough, tragedy might be just around the corner. If it is we will need to be made of some sterner metal to get through, like those commemorated and remembered here from all those years ago.

The American Monument.

Finlaggan

It is only a simple sign on the main road through Islay and you could easily miss it. It points to the west and carries the same name as the ferry we arrived on: Finlaggan. To the uninitiated this will not mean much but Finlaggan is the spiritual home of the Lords of the Isles. We take the road and after about a mile come on the Visitor Centre and can see beyond to the settlement where the Lords made their home.

The Centre is small but has all the information you might expect well displayed including some video footage. Coffee is available and there is even

The landscape and ruins at Finlaggan.

a collection of wellington boots in varied sizes you can borrow to go and have a close look at the settlement. Walkways have been laid but even so it is wet and muddy so protective gear is welcome.

Today Islay lies on the western edge of Scotland but when the Celtic saints Columba and Findlugan were talking the talk it was at the centre of a territory which included Argyllshire but also the north of Ulster in Northern Ireland. It meant that in the sixth and seventh centuries Islay and Finlaggan were at the heart of all that was going on and so were the Lords of the Isles who lived there. The territory was called Dal Riata and dates back two thousand years. The people were Gaelic speaking.

Monastic life was the driving force for the Church at that time. The monasteries continued to grow and develop until the sixteenth century when in England Henry VIII inflicted his mortal blow of dissolution. They recovered in the nineteenth century but sadly then declined in the last. There are currently some interesting alternative examples of people living in communities which are mixed, with men and women sharing the discipline of the religious life without necessarily taking life vows. So monasticism is not finished but adapting, like the rest of the Church.

It wasn't quite all plain sailing at Finlaggan either because the Vikings landed on the west coast of Scotland in the eighth century. Landed might be understating it, raided is a better description with no doubt a good deal of pillaging thrown in. They attacked the monastery on Iona on their first recorded raid in 795. The raiding eventually led to a Norse settlement on Islay and the west coast from the ninth century on. Place names reflect this today, so for example, as we learnt from our host, the "bus" in Persabus Farm where we are staying is Norse for farm or dwelling. The Norse evidently liked Islay and the islands because they were soon the dominant presence. Norway converted to Christianity around the year 1000, which may have made life easier going and acted as a unifying force with the Celts, who were already Christian. In Church terms Islay became part of the Diocese of Sodor but under the Archdiocese of Trondheim in Norway.

We pull on our wellies from those provided in the Visitor Centre and make our way to the settlement where the Lords of the Isles actually lived and kept their eye on all that was happening in Dal Riata. This settlement is on one of three islands on the loch, known as Eilean Mòr. The other two are Eilean na Comhairle at the north end and Eilean Mhuireill. Finlaggan isn't a sea loch so there is no access from here directly to open water and other parts of Dal Riata. We approach through a carpet of reeds waving in the wind and with some lilies scattered on the water. It gives a feel of hidden otherworldliness and mystery.

There is a beauty here and you can see why the Lords of the Isles chose to make it their home. The sun shines through the few clouds there are. But we can also see how exposed the site is and on a cold winter's night you only hope they could get a good fire going and keep warm. Despite the duck boarding some places en route have filled up with water and we paddle and even splash like small children having fun – Don't do that you'll get soaked!

Eilean Mòr is the biggest of the islands at just over 7000 square metres. A stone causeway would have connected it originally to the mainland but this has now been lost. The island was where the Lords lived and contained a chapel, burial site, housing and outbuildings. There would have been some kind of wooden palisade round the island and a gatehouse, all designed to heighten security and keep out anyone who might want to come pillaging with intent.

Ginny keeping her feet dry in the borrowed wellies.

The first Lord of the Isles was John I in the fourteenth century and a line of succession was established which lasted into the fifteenth century. John II was the fourth Lord but after him the title was reserved to the Crown. There was a revival of monarchy under Domhnall Dubh in the middle of the sixteenth century. Domhnall was welcomed home to Islay and to Finlaggan. Although he raised an army, when he died he had no heir and the title lapsed and the Lordship ended.

There was internal Scottish conflict between the clans, notably the MacDonalds and the Campbells and latterly with the Stewarts. There was also the continual running sore with the English. Finlaggan was significant in all this because the Lords of the Isles had established there a Council of the Isles which met on the second of the two loch islands, Eilean na Comhairle.

This is an artificial island first begun in the Stone Age and used and adapted from then right through to the 15th century. Latterly it had its own Council Chamber. The Council was made up of clan chiefs who passed laws and sorted out any bother that was brewing or had already taken off.

On Eilean Mòr there was a chapel and Great Hall and the ruins of these can still be seen. They sound grand but the impression is that life at Finlaggan was rough, ready and tough at times. This was true for everyone in that all the conveniences we are used to just didn't exist. You had to kill your own meat and grow your own veg in harsh weather and circumstances. The Lords had power over a large part of Scotland and Northern Ireland but they weren't living in luxury and had to get their hands dirty to survive as subsistence farmers and hunters.

Finlaggan is a sacred place in two ways. It is sacred because it is a window into the past. It gives an insight into where we have come from and into a very different way of life and government. There is something to be taken seriously here which stops us living too much in the present. We don't want to live in the past either but if we become consumed only with the things of the moment our feet will not be on solid ground. What the past gives is a sense of what is valuable, by treasuring great moments and movements and places which show us what it means to be human at its best. Finlaggan was a community of people managing and believing in its own identity and way of life. They cherished their Celtic and Gaelic traditions and it defined them. It gave them a sense of belonging, to each other and to the ground on which they walked. People need that. We are not just individuals adrift in the world – we belong. They knew there was a bond between them and where they lived. It made Finlaggan sacred for many.

The people who lived there also had a bond with God, which is the second way in which Finlaggan is sacred. Right at the centre of their community was a chapel they built with their own hands so that Finlaggan is a window into God, then and now. The name Finlaggan comes from St Findlugan, the early Christian missionary and contemporary of St Columba – we are talking sixth century. Christianity came to Scotland from Ireland and these were the guys who did the business and brought the message. Findlugan was the first abbot of the abbey in Tamlaght, now Ballykelly in Co. Derry. Finlaggan became a cradle of Celtic Christianity.

At the southern end of Loch Finlaggan an early medieval cast bronze figure of Christ was found which had been wrenched from a crucifix. His arms outspread on the Cross, Christ epitomises the suffering of the world which the people of Islay would have readily recognised. They saw him as a suffering God, suffering like they themselves were at times, as all people do. The Christian story and the life and death of Jesus was a way of understanding the trials of life which they were familiar with. It gave them images to hold on to – the Arrest, the Trial, the Flogging, the Cross, the Pietà, the empty tomb – which helped them find hope and to find God. A culture which has no religious myths has no way to interpret suffering, no life raft to keep it afloat, no light to follow in the darkness.

Those early believers would also have sensed the presence of the divine, as I did, in the mystery and beauty of Finlaggan itself. The reed beds and open landscape, the hills and the setting sun across the water of the loch all spoke of a presence beyond ourselves, mysterious and beautiful. This mystery, this beauty, are the face and embrace of the divine presence. They evoke God. When we love a place like Finlaggan it steals on our hearts as a piece of much loved music might. It releases our love and we have a feeling of God being by our side and our life and destiny being bound up with his. Whether Finlaggan gifts us a first-time encounter with God or nurtures a long-held faith, Finlaggan, ancient and mysterious, takes it forward and enriches our believing. We are pleased to have been here and will remember our visit when God is hard to find and the nights are long and dark.[12]

View across Finlaggan loch.

Part Three

Kindness to strangers

Service, kindness and diversity make life rich and rare.

Opposite: The Good Samaritan, stained glass window, St Mary Abbot, Kensington *iStock*

Seven: "Glasgow belongs to me"

I belong to Glasgow,
Dear old Glasgow town,
But there's something the matter with Glasgow,
For it's going round and round!
I'm only a common old workin' lad,
As anyone here can see,
But when I get a couple o' drinks on a Saturday,
Glasgow belongs to me.

Will Fyffe (1921)

We leave Islay on the ferry called *Finlaggan* but from Port Ellen in the south of the island rather than Port Askaig, where we arrived, in the north. The *Finlaggan* comes and goes from both harbours. Port Ellen is the major port of the two and is named after the wife of Walter Campbell who planned and built the village in the 1820s.

We park the hire car leaving the keys under the sun visor as instructed and, cases pulled behind us on wheels, ascend the long gangplank up to the entrance onto the ship. This is a fairly steep step at our time of life and in recognition of this metal bars have been built in to give feet something to push against in making the ascent. Cases don't do so well and bang and bump as you go, unless that is, you are a maiden in distress, like someone I know, and your man is struggling with his own luggage and not taking any notice of you. Then a burly seafarer might come to your rescue and take your case in hand and whisk it on board without a bump or a bang to be heard.

"Leave that to me, hen."

"Oh thank you very much."

We soon find seats by a window and get settled in. As we depart, we make our way outside and sit up on deck and look back at Port Ellen and Islay as we steam away. The ship's wash stretches out in a straight line behind us. We hold hands and turn up our collars against a stiff breeze.

"Would you come back again?"

"Yes, it's been magic."

Coming to Islay hadn't exactly been a pin in the map but we didn't really

know what we would find until we got here. Some years ago we had visited the islands of Skye and then Harris and Lewis to the north, the Outer Hebrides, so Islay had offered something similar but in the south, the Inner Hebrides. Guidebooks tell you so much but they can't convey atmosphere and magic which is some of what we have found here. It has been a memorable few days and something we have enjoyed and shared. They bring you together, these islands and so give a sense of contentment with the visit and with each other. We sit close on the wooden bench and look back. No need to say much as we are just happy to be with each other and to have a hand to hold. Islay has been a find and one to add to our "islands that we have loved" collection. We are thankful for times like these. They are gems to bring out and admire, photos to flip through, stories to recall and warm the heart. We are big James Taylor fans and have seen him in concert. Sitting holding hands a line from one of his songs keeps coming back to me: "My head is full of springtime and my heart is full of you". But we're getting cold so it's time to go back inside and get in the queue for a hot chocolate.

The crossing is smooth and we dock at Kennacraig where the ferry is timed to coincide with the coach coming up from Campbeltown. It will go to Inveraray, which is where we picked it up coming down, but it goes on to Glasgow. We stay on board because we have a room booked for the night at a Glasgow Travelodge.

Queen Street Station, Glasgow, where the staff looked after us.

A welcome awaits

On arriving in Glasgow, the first thing is to go to Queen Street Station and secure tickets for the next day's journey to Fort William, before moving on to our nearby Travelodge. We are rather fans of Travelodge and this one is no disappointment. The staff look after us and it has a decent restaurant and comes up with a good salad just when we need it.

On unpacking it becomes clear I have left all our travel papers and tickets in a folder at the station. Oh, for goodness sake! So, I hot foot back and thankfully the ticket office have taken them in and all is well. I seem to have the forgetting gene or maybe it is just that as you get older attention and concentration don't function as well. Either way I make a note to try harder and do better which sounds like my school report: perhaps it's been going on longer than I like to think. Opposite the Travelodge is a statue of the Duke of Wellington on a horse, standing on a plinth. It's an impressive edifice but the Iron Duke has a problem because someone has placed a large traffic cone on his head. This seems familiar and I have a memory of having seen

The Duke of Wellington keeps an eye on Glasgow

the Duke, cone and all, on television, which means the cone must have been there some time. That may be because you would need a cherry picker, or someone a good deal more nimble and agile than me, to climb up plinth, horse and the Duke before being able to reach it.

So it could be that it has become an accidental landmark. People give directions by it and have grown fond of having it around and the cone stays.

"Hey, Jock, which way to the station?"

"Next left and straight on past the Duke's head."

Or is it that the Duke with his cone has become a rallying point for Scottish independence? The council pretend not to notice and it's a poke in the eye to the English because the Duke may have been Anglo-Irish but he was, after all, a dyed in the wool pillar of the English ruling classes. Although ironically it was the Scots Greys who did the business at Waterloo and helped Wellington win the day, which is probably why he's here at all. Their cavalry charge sometime after 1.30pm on 18 June 1815 was thought by many to be a crucial turning point in the battle. Sergeant Charles Ewart of the Greys famously captured one of only two French ensigns taken on the day. The bravery and furore of the charge was in turn captured by Lady Butler in her 1881 painting *Scotland for Ever!*. So say many Scots today, but they might mean something a bit different.

The next morning we are up bright and early and make our way to Queen Street Station picking up some takeaway breakfast, as we go, from a local café. The young lady serving is very attentive: two bags in the tea or it's a bit on the weak side, she tells us. We put the takeaway cups in the carrier supplied but hang on a minute because she knows the carrier will give way like that, out comes a special tray to take the cups and take the strain. A new carrier is produced for this and another to take fruit and sandwich, our breakfast of choice this morning. We are impressed with this level of care and attention but it's slowed up the queue of office workers desperate for their own breakfasts. The line winds round the café and out the door. We beat a hasty retreat.

It's sunny and, as we enter, the station has that crisp bright confident morning feel to it. The sunlight falls in shafts through the windows. They cry out to be painted by a painter with atmosphere at the end of his or her brush. We are in good time and find seats opposite the gate where our train will arrive. Obliging Scotrail staff who man the barrier come over and, without any inquiry from us, ask if we are "all right". What with the home from home at Travelodge, the station staff looking after my lost property, café attention to detail and unsolicited concern from staff on the barrier we feel Glasgow belongs to us and is on course for European City of Kindness to Strangers. All this hidden in the everyday and ordinary. It is the day of small things but we are grateful for the hand of kindness we have experienced here. We eat breakfast and watch the commuters arriving by train for a day's work in Scotland's second city. They flood in. There isn't one black face to be seen amongst them.

Diversity

One of the key issues for the UK, and for many other countries too, is how to manage diversity. There are some who think diversity is a bad idea in the first place and there are others who welcome mixed communities with people from many countries and backgrounds living cheek by jowl. Mostly this takes place in the cities although on current showing possibly not so much in Glasgow. The truth is we work on too narrow a front. The real context isn't the ethnic mix in one country, our country, but in one world, our world. Once that is established then we see that we are all people, human beings all, made in the image of God and so brothers and sisters of one another. The problem is that difference frightens us and we back off; it creates a breakdown in family life, the human family. But if we engage, we often discover that difference is interesting and stimulating. We build bridges across divides and come closer. We become committed to each other because whatever our origin and background we are all human and made of the same stock by the one true God. When that happens a new strength and safety is established. We no longer need to live in fear but in friendship.

The resurgence of nationalism world-wide offers no long-term solution to differences that divide, only a perpetuation of many groups and factions each manning their own barricade. Faith is often part of their profile whether Christian, Muslim, Jewish or Hindu. Churches, instead of worrying about their own numbers and getting people into their way of thinking and believing – A Decade of Evangelism – could give themselves to a Decade of Understanding. It would advance their own credibility and adherence and begin to change the face of Britain for the better. We have to think in terms of what matters now and not so much what matters hereafter. God will worry about that and it can safely be left in his care.

The 2020 pandemic showed at least two things: how willing and ready many people are to serve others and extend kindness to strangers in caring for those in need, notably in hospitals and care homes. It also highlighted the way that people from many and diverse backgrounds can work together and that it is only in this way that the world can be served and the needs of people met. It's as though the hidden voice of God pleads with us to enjoy the richness of diversity and to stop making it a flash point for conflict and violence. What's wrong with you, he seems to say, can't you see it's a better way?

The Bible is keen to get this message across. In the Old Testament in the story of Ruth when there was a famine Elimelech left the land of Judah and went with his wife Naomi and their two sons to live in Moab. Sadly Elimelech died and his two sons also died. The sons had married Moabite women so this left Ruth and her two daughters-in-law Orpah and Ruth together. As they had moved back to Judah Naomi encouraged Orpah and Ruth to return to Moab, to their own country. Although Orpah went Ruth refused and made a pledge to Ruth: where you go I shall go, where you stay I shall stay. Your people will be my people; your God my God. This is a story of commitment and loyalty in a mixed marriage and between people of different countries. It transcends the immediate to emphasis our shared humanity and the bonds that tie us together.(13)

In the New Testament Jesus draws this out in his best-known parable where it is not his own people, the chosen People of Israel, who are prized and respond when calamity strikes but someone from another land and of another faith. He challenges his own people to see how people from traditions other than their own have their value and should not be dismissed out of hand, it's all part of being kind to strangers:

A lawyer once came forward to test Jesus by asking "Teacher, what must I do to inherit eternal life?" Jesus said, "What is written in the law?" He replied, "Love the Lord your God with all your heart, and with all your soul, and with all your strength, and with all your mind; and your neighbour as yourself." Jesus said "That is the right answer". Wanting to justify himself the lawyer said, "But who is my neighbour?"

Jesus replied, "A man was on his way from Jerusalem to Jericho when he was set upon by robbers, who stripped and beat him and went off leaving him half dead. It so happened that a priest was going down the same road, and when he saw him, he went past on the other side. So too a Levite came to the place, and when he saw him went past on the other side. But a Samaritan who was going that way came upon him, and when he saw him he was moved to pity. He went up and bandaged his wounds, bathing them with oil and wine. Then he lifted him on to his own beast, brought him to an inn, and looked after him. Next day he produced two silver pieces and gave them to the innkeeper, and said, 'Look after him; and if you spend more, I will repay you on my way back.' Which of these three do you think was neighbour to the man who fell into the hands of robbers?" He answered, "The one who showed him kindness." Jesus said, "Go and do as he did."[14]

Eight: The West Highland Line, Scotland's finest

It's not a long wait for our train out of Glasgow Queen Street, which is on time, and we set off on what many consider to be the most scenic railway journey in the world. Two years running it won an award with exactly that title. We find seats and settle in. Immediately the top of a bald head appears tilted back over the seat in front gazing up at the carriage roof in a fixed stare. Strewth, has he snuffed it? No, not wishing to miss any of the coming scenic view he is putting in his contact lenses and hoping, no doubt, for 20–20 vision as a result. We have reserved seats back to the engine on the righthand side as we go forward. A quick glance at our guidebook tells us that we are in the wrong place, as usual, and we really need to be facing the

The beauty of the West Highland Line from the train window.

engine on the lefthand side to take full advantage of the scenery. This is the train travelling equivalent of the pre-war cruise liner dictum: Port out Starboard home – POSH. I try hard to find an equally pleasing acronym for this train journey but without success. There seem to be plenty of seats available so we switch to the seats as advised. Posh, that's us. In these new seats we join, we think, three Germans just behind us decked out in shorts and on a biking holiday. They turn out to be Dutch and on foot which just shows how wrong you can be about other people. They are going to do 17k from the Bridge of Orchy, a station coming up on the line, including Ben Nevis which is 7k up and 7k down. They are in their forties and still have a lot of go. Across the way I get talking to him from Arizona who has flown in to Glasgow today and is making for Tyndrum, the stop before the Bridge of Orchy. He hopes to do 7k, on the West Highland Way, which for him is quite enough, thank you. He's done it before and has the measure of it.

Perhaps that's because he's older than the three from Holland so the go may not be all that it used to be. He has a small rucksack and that seems to be about it, travelling light all the way from the States. He commends a shuttle bus which goes half way up Ben Nevis. Making it three and a half kilometres to the top, which sounds about right for me.

Under the seat

A few years ago, I tried to climb Schielhallion near Rannoch, another Munro like Ben Nevis, coming in at something over 3,000 feet, but couldn't get much beyond half way, not enough puff. We were staying in Rannoch because I did a locum at the local church of All Saints. The village is separated from the station and sits isolated on Rannoch Moor. Pitlochry is an hour or so in the other direction and the nearest large town. They have a repertory theatre which is unusual today as rep has widely been replaced by touring theatre companies. However it works well there in the summer season. The show doesn't change every week but every day of the week on a seven day rotating basis. This means visitors get a new show each night, if they want one, and there's bound to be something you fancy during your stay.

We took in a show and then made our way back to Keepers Cottage at Rannoch which goes with the locum. But I had put my coat under my seat at the theatre and sad to say the house key fell out on the floor. So when we arrive ready for bed there's no key to get in and it's gone midnight. The theatre will be shut and we don't feel we can knock up a local church contact at this hour to let us in. Nothing for it but to spend the night in the car overlooked by Schielhallion keeping a watchful eye on wayward visitors. We hope for better luck tonight in Fort William.

Added value

One of the attractions of travel, and especially travel abroad, is to be found in the differences in the landscapes you discover compared to the place you call home. For those who live in the flat lands of Holland the mountains and hills of Scotland must promise a whole new world where life will seem sweeter and the air fresher. If the deserts of Arizona are where you come from (they have four deserts each receiving less than ten inches of rain a year) the green grass of the West Highland Way will seem like heaven on earth. There life will surely be richer and more verdant just like the vegetation.

The physical landscape and the human landscape each bring their own

All the way from Arizona.

richness and go hand in hand. To this may be added the culture of the country you are visiting. There's nothing like the pipes and the kilt. They are the hallmarks of what it means to be Scottish and distinguish the Scots as a people in their own right with their own way of life. Even the calamities of travel have their place because losing your key and locking yourself out of your holiday home makes the visit memorable and marks it in the annals of family history. "Remember when" brings a warm glow once you are back home. There is added value hidden within difference and calamity. Perhaps God is at work when life is on the move.

The Bridge of Orchy

Conductor of the Year

Although we have booked to Fort William, the West Highland Line goes further, all the way to Mallaig. We look at doing this last bit on The Jacobite which is a heritage steam train that has a schedule of trips from Fort William. It was The Jacobite that appeared in the Harry Potter movies as the Hogwarts Express. It has made the line and the train famous with all true HP believers.

It is about another hour and a half's journey on from Fort William to Mallaig. Google tells us The Jacobite is fully booked tomorrow so when the conductor comes round we buy tickets to stay on this train all the way to Mallaig and come back to Fort William for the night after that. The conductor, who we learn from her name badge is called Susie, says it is better with Scotrail anyway – no smoke in your eyes and it's fifty quid cheaper, so who's arguing with that.

Susie turns out to be good news. She takes a personal interest in the passengers and regularly stops to chat. This is her train and she likes to make everyone feel welcome. Which is a cut above many lines and conductors that we have known. When we reach Corrour a lot of people pile off. Only one middle door opens here because of a short platform so they are all coming our way. Gangway! Here comes Susie at the run anxious to get to the door to help people off.

"Excuse, excuse I'm coming throoooooough."

On the platform she is friendly and interested in all who are leaving, "Oh hello again" as she recognises someone from a previous trip. She even takes photos for a group of not so young men who pose by the station name board to prove they have been there. We learn there is a lake nearby and about a nine mile circular route round it to pick up the train on its return. They get a wave goodbye and the train sets off again as we settle down waiting for Mallaig to put in an appearance. Susie comes to see if we are all OK and asks if we mind if she closes the window as it can be a bit draughty with it open. She has our welfare at heart.

"Tickets pleeeeeease."

I doze off... suddenly it all starts happening, dogs start barking, the passengers start getting up, camera phones at the ready, and looking out the windows. Here comes Susie on the run again to give notice over the PA to

The Glenfinnan Viaduct

make sure no one misses the moment. We are approaching the Glenfinnan Viaduct. This is where The Jacobite really came into its own in all its steaming splendour as the Hogwarts Express. Everyone wants a photo to send to their grandchildren, us included. It is now known by aficionados as the Harry Potter Viaduct. It is a fab bit of railway architecture and you want to send up a drone to get that long distant shot of the train as it comes round the curve in the track. Here we go!

South of the border there has been a long-running dispute between the unions and some rail companies over guards, in Scotland known as conductors. "Keep the Guard on the Train" is the rallying cry from the union and you can get badges with those words on to wear in support. The rationale from the union's point of view has centred around safety and, of course, jobs. The companies think driver-only trains are the way to go. There is a case to be made for efficiency and keeping costs down. What our experience here suggests is that there is another aspect as well. It is that taking a journey isn't just a matter of getting from A to B and putting up with all the stress that might involve. A journey can be a pleasure and you shouldn't only find that on an up-market cruise liner. It is part of what offering a service, especially a public service, is all about.

Our conductor, Susie, has an approach that puts that into practice. It's the difference between getting a meal from a machine – put in your money, press the button and out comes a sandwich, a drink and change, if you're lucky – and going to a restaurant and receiving attention from a staff that knows how to make you feel at home and relaxed and wanting to come back. They are helpful and welcoming and the meal is well presented and prepared. We expect it when we go out to eat. It can be the same when we go out to travel. It is treating people like human beings not parcels in transit.

It's that "me – me" culture again where it is easy to lose sight of service to others as part of what makes life worthwhile. This isn't demeaning to those who offer that service. It isn't a return to the age of deference, forelock touching and knee bending. Good service brings respect to those who give it as well as to those who receive it. That's what we have seen today on the West Highland Line and it has made the journey that much more pleasurable, stress free and enhanced even the magnificent scenery of loch and seascape, glen and mountain, viaduct and all things Harry Potter. Service may not get your name in lights but, hidden though it often is, it brings its own dignity and creates its own sense of worth. Susie certainly gets my vote for Conductor of the Year.

> *A jealous dispute broke out [among the disciples]: who among them should rank the greatest? Jesus said, "In the world, kings lord it over their subjects. Not so with you: on the contrary, the highest among you must bear himself like the youngest, the chief of you like a servant. For who is greater – the one who sits at table or the servant who waits on him? Surely the one who sits at table. Yet here I am among you as one who serves."*[15]

Keep the Guard on the Train!

Admiring the view

There's much to admire in the landscape we see out the train window but there's also a human landscape to admire as well. It's always the odd and glorious which seem to catch my eye. A middle-aged couple, he in baggy shorts and she in a denim dress from the sixties catches my eye. They took over the seats forsaken by the Dutch walkers. They have two dogs with them, terriers who they bring on board in a push chair but are transferred to laps for the journey. These are the barking dogs of the Harry Potter Viaduct. It's time for food and the dogs get a look in but are reprimanded and told "Not to eat other people's food" because "they know every word we say". What can a good dog do? One minute you're the baby of the family with your own push chair and sitting on laps, the next it's back to run of the mill dog food like any mongrel on the street.

We've been on the train for a while now and I decide to stretch my legs and do a bit more people watching. I plonk down in another carriage. The man across the aisle looks a real tough nut and someone you wouldn't want to meet on a dark night: an Al Pacino lookalike with wild dark hair and donkey jacket. He must at least, I decide, be part of organised crime in Scotland and on his way to collect protection money from the good folks of Fort William. But hang on a minute; a closer look reveals he is surreptitiously eating a bar of Cadbury's chocolate. Sneaking a piece at a time when no one is looking. What a softy. I thought I was the only one who sneaked a bar of Cadbury's when no one's looking but I guess it must be going on all over the country, to Cadbury's great relief, and tough nuts included.

Then here's another bloke, a hoody, knocking back lager from the bottle. In between swigs he begins to prepare a roll-up. He has a pouch of tobacco. He reaches into his pocket for something else. Cannabis? No it's a filter to be added on health and safety grounds. But surely he's not going to light up here? No, he's getting ready. He's gasping and getting off at the next stop and so he is making sure he is well prepared so no time will be lost. Ah! that's better.

Further up the carriage four old guys like me are sat round a table. Opposite them an attractive middle age woman is struggling to get her case out of the luggage rack. One of the old guys gets up to help. She thanks him and gives him a winning smile. He sits down again as she leaves and all eyes are on him.

"What?"

"You're working well"

"I was just giving her a hand"

"That's what we're worried about"

"Oh, for goodness sake"

But what of the scenery that this line is famous for and we have been admiring out the window? Like Islay it surprises you and catches you out when you least expect it. The train moves at a sedate pace because the track winds and twists to fit the landscape. This is never going to be HS3. The wheels make that clickety clack repetitive sound that used to be part of every rail journey, until longer rails were introduced for a smoother ride. Suddenly you are round another bend and Wow! The land dips away from the line and a loch and glen open up with mountains rising in the background. Will you look at that!

This is a landscape of contrasts. The glens are soft and gentle. The rain makes them green and full of life. The mist may swirl in the valleys in the early morning, but the warmth of the bright morning sun soon dispels the cloud. There is a joy and exuberance to be had walking here. You could grasp a new confidence, a new realisation of hope, a shedding of despair that might otherwise pull you down. Life is for living and being here affirms it. You stride out certain you will reach your destination.

Then as you look up there are the hills and mountains reaching above you ragged and challenging in their grandeur. These too resonate with the lives we lead. We know the ragged pathways only too well; the challenges that come our way in relationships or over health or the loss of loved ones. Can these challenges be climbed and scaled like those distant slopes and peaks? Life is also for overcoming and we honour those who do so: those who have faced great adversity or suffering, those who have lived their lives for others and against self-interest, those who have shown courage and endurance.

Then there are the trees and lochs we pass. These are places to rest a while and refresh. We know the early morning mists don't always clear and the mountains can't always be climbed. Instead what we need are places to stop and be sustained and to recover. The lapping waters of the lochs and the shade of the trees present the opportunity we need to do just that. We step aside. This isn't always admired or recognised, taking a break. We are too hard on ourselves and forget to be as kind to ourselves as to those around us. But it's why Sundays were originally days of rest and not frantic dashing round the shops; it's why the French like long lunch hours and the Spanish take siestas; it's why British prizing of hard work is good as far as it goes, until it goes too far.

The scenery we see has a beauty and a magnificence all its own. It has its own aesthetic appeal like the great work of art it is. And if we will let it it picks up the pace and opportunities of the lives we live. It reminds us where our future lies and what matters most. In all this it is God's creation we see made and shaped by his own hand. Not in any crude creationist way do we see this. Nature has its own integrity and importance. We don't need to deny how it came to be and how it works to admire it or to see the divine hand at play. The crisis of our generation is that we thwart it and exploit it. It is why we are desperately trying to respond to the climate crisis we see all around us before it is too late. Unbeknown to us we will see this response in action when we arrive at Fort William.

Magnificent and glorious

We undercut the symbolic importance of nature and creation when we are blind to the messages written by a hidden divine hand in the natural world around us. God comes to us in and through his creation. It is the way he speaks. It is why creation is sacramental. Bread and wine remind us of The Last Supper that Jesus shared with his disciples. We share them in remembrance of him. Lochs and glens, hills and mountains also speak if we have ears to hear. Life can simply be *seen* as pragmatic and taken at face value, it is what it is. Or, we *understand* that part of the glory and magnificence of the natural world is that it is a window through which we *see* God and find him for ourselves.

It is the God who inspires and brings new hope. It is the God who enables us to overcome and go on and it is the God who brings the rest and refreshment we need to sustain us on the journey. If diversity and difference is an issue, through his creation God seems to say that it is in the contrasts that his glory and ours are to be found. It is the diversity that makes creation magnificent and glorious. If the landscape on earth was like the landscape on Mars, all of a kind, so much would be lost. It is the differences we cherish, in the landscape itself and in the people who walk upon it.

Mallaig

At Mallaig there is time to get off and look round before returning on the next train to Fort William. A local shop acts as a left luggage office for a small fee so we ditch our cases and wander around. Mallaig has a good harbour and is the main fishing port of the west coast. You suspect that the fishing is not what it used to be but a local shopkeeper still offers genuine oak smoked kippers.

Education here is different from much of the rest of the UK. Children who live on the islands have to come and lodge here, because of the distance from home to secondary schools. There is no just walking down the road and round the corner as I did. Some schools teach Scottish Medium Education which means the pupils are taught in Gaelic, allowing other schools to teach in English. Mallaig is also a centre for distance learning and has a fine college which is reported to be one of the most successful of its kind in Britain with a strong local take up.

All this is not immediately apparent to the day visitor. Tourists don't see or appreciate what goes on for locals. They are not on holiday but getting on with everyday life. It's hidden, as you might say, like learning itself. And education isn't just a passport to open a door to a job or career because at its best it also shapes who you are. It is part of the creative and hidden hand of God enabling and developing our skills and personalities.

From Mallaig you can access by ferry the Isle of Skye and the small Hebridean islands of Rum, Eigg, Muck and Canna. This immediately brings into view the romantic story of Bonnie Prince Charlie, commemorated in the Skye Boat Song:

Mallaig Harbour

Speed bonny boat like bird on the wing
Onward the sailors cry
Carry the lad born to be King
Over the sea to Skye.

Prince Charles Edward Stuart was the grandson of James II. He hoped to challenge and defeat George II and had led an army of 6,000 against the English as far as Derby. But he was defeated at the Battle of Culloden in 1746. His tactics were flawed. He rejected the advice of his army commanders and this exposed his men to the forces of the Duke of Cumberland. The Duke became known as "The Butcher" for the alleged atrocities his men committed when pursuing the Jacobite army in retreat.

It was after this the Bonnie Prince made his escape from Scotland with the help of loyal supporters who refused to betray him, even though there was a reward of £30,000 for doing so. Of these Flora MacDonald is the most famous. She took Charlie by boat safely over the sea to Skye disguised as her maid Betty Burke. From there the Young Pretender eventually reached France. The Jacobite cause was lost and Charlie spent the rest of his life in continental Europe.

We mooch around the gift and clothing shops of Mallaig wistfully looking over to Skye. We picture the man on whom many hopes and dreams rested making his way there, in the prow of Flora's boat as she lay on the oars, knowing the dream was over and the hope gone. Here was an assertion of Scottish independence and a early reminder that Scotland has always been a country with its own spirit and identity – more of which later. Back down to earth the enticing aroma of fish and chips is in the air and smells good, but we resist and settle for tea and a sandwich, boring, before boarding the train again having retrieved our cases. So Fort William, let's be having you.

Loch Eilt Causeway *With Permission West Coast Railways*

Beasdale *With Permission West Coast Railways*

GET OFF THE
COUCH
AND REDUCE EMISSIONS

Stop
building
crap
houses

NO NATURE
=
NO FUTURE
KEEP THE O
THE SOIL

ICE CREAM FUDGE & COFFEE
FOR THE
PLANET
ACT NOW
GLOBAL CLIMATE
STRIKE
SCHOOL STRIKE
FOR THE
CLIMATE

PLANET
FUTURE
NO PLANET
B

SCHOOL + WORK STRIKE
CLIMATE + ECOLOGICAL EMERGENCY
ACT NOW

Part Four
On the streets where we live

God comes alive on the streets of our towns and cities and in the lives of the people who live there

Opposite: School Strike Day, Fort William 2019

Nine: Fort William, lost and found

We arrive at Fort William and walk up from the station to the High Street which has been pedestrianised. Before looking for our bed for the night we plonk down in a small park just off on the left hand side. Jimmy joins us. We have never met Jimmy before but he begins talking. He's out for a walk. He usually walks with a friend but he couldn't make it today. When they meet Jimmy's friend always asks "Where are we going today?" but then heads off on a route of his own choosing. Jimmy says he gets his way about one in ten; he's feeling a bit hard done by.

I say "Well, if he chooses the route perhaps he should buy the drinks?"

"Well, he could do that right enough, he's rolling in it."

"Where is he today?"

"He's with his woman. I introduced them. He's just made his will and left it all to her."

"What no family?"

"No, no family at all."

"Not left it all to you then?"

"That'll be the day."

"Sounds as though she's onto a good thing."

"You can say that again."

We didn't book with Travelodge this time but thought we would give the local hostel a go. We find it on the High Street. There is no lift from the ground floor to reception on the first floor so there is a good deal of huffing and puffing to get our two overfull cases up the stairs. We do them one at a time with bent backs and plenty of lifting and pushing between us like trying to get an obstinate mule along a dusty road. But a welcome awaits and we find our room. Thankfully, there is a lift to our floor from reception and we plonk down gratefully on the bed. There are three beds altogether: a double and two singles. We go for the double, romantics that we are, which affords a decent view onto the estuary. The room is basic but fine for the couple of nights we shall be here. We unpack a bit, and go back down to the High Street looking for food.

Wetherspoons

Walking along we consult menus outside restaurants on the way but in the end the local Wetherspoons at the top of the High Street proves irresistible. It's dead cheap of course but we quite like the atmosphere too. It's called here The Great Glen which is just up the road and runs from Inverness to Fort William taking in Nessie and Loch Ness on the way. We like Wetherspoons

because there are always people coming and going. It gives a feeling of being alive and you never know who you might meet. These are ordinary people like us, here for a cheap meal and a fun evening, if they can get it. Any minute a hen night could arrive in bunny ears and garish outfits, balloons flying, in fits of laughter and talking at the tops of their voices. We go for the curry.

Tonight it's quite international, with a showing of Chinese people, although everyone is extremely white. A family of six claim a table near us and our menu too. They then begin to work out their order. This is not as simple as you might think. It goes on for a long time; much wrangling and changing of minds. So much so that Mum can't stand it any longer. She gets up and begins to put her coat on. She's off. She has been here too many times before. They can never decide and she's got the hump. Calm down, mother. Finally it's settled and Dad goes off to order from the bar, he's paying, as usual.

The ordering works well. You go to the bar and they put it all on screen which whizzes through to the kitchen, who knock it out in no time, and it arrives at your table. There's no more of that shouting to the cooks that used to be the chain of command: "Two medium cod, one small chips, one large chips, one with onion rings, one without". This pre-dates modern technology but had its appeal. It relied on human technology and the cooks remembering what had been ordered, which was a skill of their trade. The trouble with on-screen ordering is that you have to have exactly what's there, nothing less and nothing more, otherwise the technology can't cope. So, when I ask for two scoops of ice cream, instead of the usual one on the menu, they each arrive in separate bowls because one scoop is the norm and that's how it's done. No matter, both scoops go the way of all flesh in the end. Thank you very much. That will do nicely, time for bed.

Direct action

The next day is School Strike Day in support of action on climate change. Greta Thunberg has inspired her generation to get out on the streets and here they are. Her story is told in the film *I am Greta* which follows her life in 2019. It is impressive because we see a sixteen-year-old school girl with Asperger's, which she openly talks about, taking the adult world to task over the climate crisis. She is invited to many countries and conferences around the world. This includes a UN Climate Conference in New York. To this she refuses to fly because it's flight and its carbon emissions which are doing the damage. Instead she goes in a racing yacht across the Atlantic and it takes two weeks. The yacht has only rudimentary facilities and not much room for moving about. Because of her Asperger's Greta is someone who likes to have well-oiled routines. These are disrupted in this crossing and she is uncomfortable and exposed to all the elements. Her dad goes with her. They brave the crossing and receive a hero's welcome as they come into New York. Watching it you can't but be moved by their courage and inspiration. Greta has been the trigger for a movement around the world, She has brought together people from many different backgrounds and races. It is a microcosm of how the world ought to be, with divisions put aside and instead the bond and embrace of friendship, and all to save the planet we share.

It's this bond which has brought children and adults together and onto the streets in Fort William. This is a school strike and it's the young people who lead the way. They are like Greta herself. They don't mince their words or shy away from telling the adult world to get its act together, it has failed for far too long with compromise and empty promises. The adults, parents and teachers, are in support so hopefully the kids won't get a row when they get back to school. There are plenty of banners in evidence:

Keep the oil in the soil – Stop building crap houses – Get off the couch and reduce emissions – For the planet act Now –
School + Work Strike 4 The Climate.

Angus is one of the first up. "Hello, I'm sixteen. I'm here because I'm fed up with spending millions on space trying to get to other planets when we are buggering up the one we've got."

There are kids of all ages including a baby in arms breast feeding as mother sits on the ground. The speakers are impressive and direct. It takes the young to cut away all the ifs and maybes and to get to the point. An articulate fourteen-year-old says it is all too urgent not to act. She invites adults to also have a say.

One of the long in the tooth says it is not just about stopping doing things but moving to a better future. It will be *better* with electric cars, *better* with insulated houses. It's a positive, as well as preserving and maintaining what we've got.

Another says: "I'm from California. My husband and I are eighty. Our Governor is taking on the President. Hoorah! We stand with you in what you are doing today." Her husband looks on beaming broadly with approval. He is enjoying being there with her and takes a special pleasure in hearing his wife speak. This marriage looks like a gem; it's one of those with bucket loads of mutual respect and appreciation. More cheers, this time for happy married life. All marriages don't have to be a rerun of *EastEnders*, I'm pleased to say.

An older man steps forward with an XR (Extinction Rebellion) symbol stuck to his forehead. He says he used to be part of the problem but has changed his ways, and now he blames God. Someone's to blame but I couldn't quite see how it was God. He gave us a planet in pretty pristine if primeval condition and, as Angus put it, is us who have buggered it up.

Extinction Rebellion stickers abound not only on foreheads but on backs, and fronts and bald heads as well. Everyone gets a round of applause. It's a fun atmosphere but it creates a stir on the High Street. You have to be a special kind of politician if you are going to listen to voices on the street and, too often, they simply get ignored. But this is why protests get going. In a democracy, in theory, everyone gets a say but you have to attract a good deal of attention to be heard. That's why XR have gone down the direct-action route, to make people, politicians in particular, listen. In a totalitarian state no one gets a say and a word out of turn gets you in trouble. The facts and figures presented by XR are both convincing and disturbing. This is what they want to get across. They are right to try and take the initiative, to be heard, but it is an uphill task. Even if the UK meets its deadlines it is hard to see how the rest of the world to a man, woman and child will do the same. It's a huge ask. The future doesn't look rosy and the consequences are far reaching. Many predictions are cataclysmic.

We went on an XR protest in London when they blocked the roads and stopped the traffic, direct action to draw attention. There is a fine balance to be struck. A later demo in east London stopped the tube running, just as people were trying to get to work, by protestors sitting on the roof of the train. You could imagine this working in middle class west London and the commuters there understanding and being sympathetic: "No, please go ahead, I completely understand, don't mind us". In working class Canning Town the man on the train roof was soon dragged down without ceremony and you could almost hear someone say: "Get the f— off or I'll break your arm". Reflecting later XR got the message and realised that part of the battle is not just getting people to listen but getting them on your side. You probably don't do that by making them late for work.

So secular protest though it is, can God be said to be involved in action to save the planet, his planet, and attempts to address climate change?

In the Bible when Moses brought the People of Israel out of slavery in Egypt, the People were happy to leave until it all started going pear-shaped. It was known as the Exodus and it was a big moment. They had been in a foreign country for over four hundred years. They didn't like it and they wanted out. But they didn't get a quick bus to the Promised Land. It took forty years, which were spent wandering in the desert. The People turned on Moses: This is another fine mess you've got us into. They didn't threaten to break his arm as far as we know but they did say: Why have you brought us out here into this wilderness where we shall probably all starve to death? We were better off in slavery in Egypt. Some people are never satisfied. It is then that God intervenes and provides manna in the wilderness for the people to eat. The story leads on to Mount Sinai, the sacred mountain, and the giving of the Ten Commandments and the sense of God's hand being upon the People.

The Bible writes up the history of the People of Israel with God in mind and speaks of him acting in his own right and name. But had you been a reporter at the time from the world's press you may not have seen it that way. You would instead have reported a gargantuan struggle between a people in slavery in Egypt under their leader Moses and a monarch, Pharaoh, who had other ideas and wanted to keep them as a cheap source of labour. Time and again Moses says: Let my people go. Time and again Pharaoh says "yes" but then changes his mind. Until the people finally break out, the Red Sea is breached, and the people are free. The Bible sees it as God in action. The reporter didn't mention God. Two different views of the same event.

That can be said of the climate change protest movement. It too is a secular debate and sometimes a confrontation between protestors and the government of the day. At the same time it can for believers be the way that God is at work to save the planet, his precious creation. That's the way he works. Lavinia Byrne in describing the Nativity puts it like this: "The simplicity of the gospel is deceptive for it is determined to show us that God uses the ordinary things of human life – like a census or a crowded inn – to break through to us".[16]

The words you use to describe what is going on depend on your point of view. The Bible uses the words of faith and we can do the same. Others will describe it differently. God is hidden in the world. He's not blatant or brash. He is often understated more than sensational. He isn't pushy or egocentric. He's often suffering and on the edge. Those who, as Jesus said, have eyes to see and ears to hear will recognise his handwriting when they read it.

Religious people can shut themselves up in an enclosed world of their own and think they are the only ones God is concerned about. Or they can take a risk and be engaged with the world and be part of world history and development. They know God cares for all the people of the world and has not withdrawn his interest or involvement whether they speak his name or not. His vision is much bigger. That is why on a summer morning in a small Scottish town our hearts were glad and rejoiced to see a protest on the streets for a cause that needs more prominence and needs to be heard. It was for us God at work, even though his name was hardly mentioned, the hidden God, and it is the way in which his voice is being raised over a crisis that has disaster written all over it. It is fast becoming the most critical debate of our age and it is why the Church should be out there fighting for urgent and immediate response to the tragedy that confronts us.

The strength and conviction of any institution is to be found in its ability to respond to the needs of the people around it and the world they live in. Many churches have now adopted eco-friendly policies about how they conduct themselves. Christian Climate Action (CCA) is a direct-action group working with the Extinction Rebellion movement. Their recently published *Time to Act* (SPCK) recounts with both passion and conviction what it means for Christians to be involved with a wider group of people with religious faith and with none. CCA have achieved credibility within the movement as a whole and flown the flag for Christian concern and determination. A church that is too often preoccupied with itself will not be taken seriously. A servant church will be working and acting on behalf of others and the needs they have. CCA are just that. Nowhere is the need for direct action more apparent at the moment than on the issue of climate change. It has taken an insignificant school girl from Sweden to bring this to the world's attention.

Ben Nevis from Loch Linnhe

Union or independence, then and now

We go to the visitor information centre to enquire about the bus, recommended by our man from Arizona, that goes up Ben Nevis. But sad to say they tell us no buses are allowed on the sacred mount so it must have been a phantom bus of the imagination. Instead we get the N47 which takes us out to Banavie Station and the further side of Loch Linnhe which lies below Ben Nevis. Except that it doesn't because I don't ring the bell in time and we sail on by. So we have to walk back a way before coming to the Caledonian Canal at Banavie.

Here there is a flight of nine locks. These are proper locks that require a lock keeper with the keys to operate them, rather than do it yourself, like the locks I am used to on the Thames. There are 29 locks altogether on the canal: slightly less than the 32 James Wall predicted would be needed in his survey of 1774. The Caledonian Canal is part of the network which connects Inverness, in the east, to Fort William, in the west, and takes in Loch Ness but also Loch Dochfour, Loch Oich and Loch Lochy on the way. It led William

Fraser, a later proponent of the scheme, to say that "nature had finished more than half of it already". The canal was needed in the eighteenth century to enable shipping, especially the fishing industry vessels of the day, to pass east–west by a short cut and not have to go by the sometimes dangerous sea routes, around Orkney.

The end of the eighteenth century was a time when the Highlands were depressed following the Clearances, in which many were deprived of their livelihood. The landowners had turned vast areas over to sheep farming, putting men out of work. In addition, laws had been introduced to ban the wearing of tartan, playing the bagpipes, and speaking Gaelic, if you can believe it. Many people emigrated to Canada. Thomas Telford came on board and in a report published in 1802 showed how a programme of public works including canal, road and bridge building would bring back jobs to the Highlands. An Act of Parliament was passed in 1803 to allow this to happen and a government grant of £20,000 allocated, evidence perhaps of the guilt felt by some for giving the Highlands a hard time. The final cost of building the canal would be over £400,000. Further government funding was to emerge, and shares were sold to make up the shortfall. Thomas Telford was appointed to get the work done.[17]

History matters. I used to think the problem with Ireland was the Irish and hence the Troubles. When I went to Ireland, I could see all too clearly how wrong and arrogant I was. It was the English that were the problem and all that they had inflicted on the Irish people. It included the government of the day's indifference to the Irish potato famine in the nineteenth century when many starved. No wonder Home Rule became the cry. It still might not have gone through in the 1920s if after the Easter Rising the British government had not shot those who defended the GPO building, one of whom was tied to a chair. It outraged the people and separation was inevitable.

The same is true of Scotland. When you go to Scotland you can see it is in every sense a long way from Westminster. Scotland has a strong culture and way of life of its own, just like Ireland, even if the English Parliament did at one time try to rub it out. Intolerance of diversity has been around a long time. Is it any wonder that large numbers of Scottish people want to be independent of the UK when you look at how the English treated their ancestors?

You can argue it was all a long time ago and we should all move on. But it isn't all a long time ago, it is also current, as the debacle over Brexit has shown, with the indifference of Westminster to Scotland's wish to stay in the EU. It is true it doesn't help anyone to bear a grudge for ever. There are too many voices raised in the world to say I have to do it "my way", when what we need is more partnership and co-operation, more joint working and respect. That is why I would still back the Union and being part of the EU. But you can see why many Scots beg to differ as far as their country is concerned.

What price unity, what price diversity?

Independence will be hard to resist, even if the Prime Minister of the day won't agree, because the support for a second referendum at the present time is growing. It is also the case that that support for the Union is strongest amongst older people who anno domini will catch up with all too soon. As with Brexit whether the outcome will be quite what everyone thinks it will be remains to be seen. The practical implications of Brexit received all too little profile in the debate which revolved around big-brush-stroke issues like sovereignty and independence. Scottish fishermen, like most of the UK fishing industry, backed Brexit but then lost out when a deal was finally done. They have paid a heavy price and feel hard done by. If Scotland goes independent it might find, in a similar way, that practical implications come to the surface which had not been anticipated, for example, a loss of employment, with the likely closure of the Faslane naval base, and the need to handle directly immigration and free movement from the EU.

In the Old Testament the People of Israel see themselves as distinctive and especially chosen by God. The Promised Land is their land. Other nations do not have this special place and are not the apple of his eye in the way they are. This leads to a "them and us" kind of culture.

The breakthrough comes in the New Testament with the coming of Jesus. He runs into conflict with his own people because he is open and accessible to all. The point about the Good Samaritan is that he was not Jewish but it is he who shows kindness to strangers and is commended by Jesus for doing so – unlike the Jewish Levite and Priest who pass by on the other side.

All this was pretty strong and controversial stuff in his day and still is today. Jesus strongly upheld the Jewish tradition in which he stood, even though he tried to reform it. He had a larger vision than the establishment of his day. Diversity doesn't mean trying to make everyone the same or amalgamating different traditions or prizing one tradition more than others. It means prizing all traditions and faiths and cultures so that each has air to breathe and there is mutual respect and they can live together.

This is true at an individual level, but it is also true between nation states and between the countries that make up the United Kingdom. Inclusion and mutuality are difficult roads to walk down. But that is the road that we always need to find if conflict is to be replaced by a recognition that we are one people on earth, a common humanity. We may be different, look different, speak different but we are brothers and sisters too, we are all *Homo sapiens*, we all have the same heavenly Father. St Paul draws this out when he writes to the church in Galatia:

> *You are all people of God in union with Christ Jesus. Baptised into union with him, you have all put on Christ as a garment. There is no such thing as Jew and Greek, slave and free, male and female; for you are all one person in Christ Jesus.*[18]

Sometimes it is only if we, like Paul, are willing to lay down our lives in small ways and in great that unity can be achieved, and peace maintained. It won't bring us fame or fortune but it might mean we are true to ourselves and true to what it really means to be human. It is reaching out across divides. It is going the second mile. It is overcoming hurt and mistrust. Which is easy to say and pontificate about; it's not easy to live out in practice. It is why long-running conflicts are so hard to resolve, because layer upon layer of mistrust has built up. Very big steps are needed to restore trust and recognise the grievances there are on both sides.

Thankfully, in the United Kingdom the level of conflict over independence hasn't reached the depth it has in some parts of the world, and did for a time in Ireland, although the same issues are at play. Despite what I have argued I recognise that sometimes a separation has to be made for liberation and development to be real. It is like the need we all have to leave home and stand on our own two feet. Sometimes it is leaving which must rule the day and independence is the only route to take. Sometimes it is continuing partnership and union that is in everybody's interest. There may be an alternative to independence for Scotland, like federation, that would carry support. As always one option has to be weighed against another and a judgement made. Only the Scottish people can and should decide their own future and the way they want to go whether that is to be independence or in partnership with the other countries of the UK.

Lost and found

Back to the trivial things of life which nearly push you over the edge: the other thing that happened in Fort William was that I lost my mobile phone and Ginny lost an earring, both on the High Street. We do a close inspection for the earring. As the street is pedestrianised there is no traffic to dodge as we do so. Although we don't actually get down on our hands and knees we must look like those police officers you see when a crime has been committed, looking for clues with big sticks and pushing at the ground and turning everything over as they do so. Maybe a crime has been committed and there is a phantom earring nicker abroad in Fort William. Sadly, no sign of the earring and we retire to Wetherspoons – again.

The phone is more difficult.

"When did you last have it?"

"In the park, I think."

"Where was it?"

"In the rucksack, front pocket."

"Did you do up the zip?"

"Well..."

It's late but I go and look on the bench in the park where we sat a while and talked with Jimmy. No luck. Time has marched on; shops are now closed and bed beckons. The anxieties begin. I have online banking on the phone. What if someone has nicked it, can they access our money? Should I phone NatWest and get them to stop everything just in case? No, it probably fell out in the bookshop; that's where it will be, they'll have it for sure. I put the rucksack down on the floor to look at a book I fancied. Tossing and turning and going over it means it's a long night.

Eventually dawn breaks and we go to the bank. No need to worry, your password will secure everything. I should have known that. On to the bookshop which is still closed but the door is open. I venture in.

"Hello, anyone there?"

After a few more Hellos a lady appears from the back but no they haven't come across a mobile. We try the Information Centre just in case but it's no again. The police are polite, but they know nothin'.

I haven't had this phone long and it's an advance on a previous one that just did pay as you go calls. No, I don't need a smart phone thank you very much. I don't want to become a phone zombie like the rest of the population. But the truth is I have now become rather wedded to this phone and I like the apps. It has become part of me. I feel lost and bereft and not a little vulnerable without it. It's like an old friend has passed on. This is a real sob story.

But it is a story with a happy ending, I am pleased to say. Ginny had earlier rung my phone so that if it was nearby, we could hear it and be reunited. Later when we are back on the train, and have left Fort William reconciled to not ever seeing my phone again, how sad is that, Ginny discovers a phone call she doesn't recognise on her phone and then a voice mail. Can you believe it but someone has found the phone and made contact because Ginny's number has shown up. Yes she will return it and we give our home address for her to do that and promise reimbursement of all expenses incurred. Profuse thanks and pledges of good will.

We rest assured. But wait a minute, is this a scam? Nicking phones then finding out addresses so they can rob your house knowing you're not there. But we live 300 miles away. Are they downloading information about us? Will I be all over Facebook and exploited for ever more? It can't be, and it isn't. How paranoid can you get?

When we return home the phone arrives in the post, safe and sound. My phone! You have returned to me and all is well. There is a note included:

Hello from Fort William. Here is your phone as promised; I am just sorry I took a wee while to send it. I charged it for you and do not worry I did not touch anything on it.

I sincerely hope everything arrived intact. Anyway, I'm glad that you'll finally get your phone back.

Good luck!

Marie

Despite pressing her about sending dosh Marie won't hear of it and no address is forthcoming. This is yet another example on our trip of the kindness of strangers and of just how goodhearted people can be. There seems to be a continual supply of stories about people who are out to get you or scam you and each other. But the truth is that even if there are some baddies there are many others who are decent and good and know how to be kind and generous and do as they would be done by. Their actions often go unseen and unreported. They prefer to stay in the shadows and incognito. Thank you, Marie, for being one of them.

The pipes and the kilt at the Edinburgh Tattoo.

Ten: Edinburgh, the city of dreams

Edinburgh is the city of our dreams because we were married here at St Thomas' Church in Corstorphine, on the road to Glasgow, all those years ago. The reception was held in a hotel on the North Bridge, now the Hilton. Ginny's mum, Vera, had booked another venue nearer to the church but at the last minute they decided they were double booked and couldn't oblige. This was undoubtedly an "Oh sod it" moment. Vera was a good knitter but every so often she would drop a stitch and then say "Oh sod it". More than a stitch had been dropped here but, formidable woman that she was, a new hotel was found and all was well. So on the day, from the outer suburbs we came right into the city centre. It gave us the pleasure of driving back down

Princes Street, in our going away gear, to go on honeymoon near Inverness. We imagined the crowds cheering on either side of the road like we were a royal procession passing on its way. There was a cheer in our hearts. Love was young and in the air.

It had been around for some time in my head if nowhere else. When I first started work I used to catch a 441 bus from outside a record shop called Record Wise which took a wise old owl as its logo. There weren't logos in those days but I remember a stuffed owl featuring in the shop displays. This was when vinyl was king and when records were really records. Vinyl, I am pleased to note, is making a comeback. In the window of Record Wise they featured Bob Dylan's *The Freewheelin' Bob Dylan* centre stage: his second studio album, released in 1963. It contained some of Dylan's early classics: "Blowin' In The Wind" and "Don't Think Twice, It's All Right". I didn't even have a record player then but I gazed longingly in the window and coveted the image if not the record. On the front cover was good old Bob mincing along a street in New York with a girl on his arm. I wanted that arm to be mine with the girl of my dreams. The girl on the cover was Suze Rotolo and she really was Bob's girl. They lived just round the corner from where the picture was taken. The image broke new ground in that it is casual and informal and in contrast to covers at the time which mostly featured much more formal poses of the bands to be found inside the sleeve.

The girl of my dreams was "the girl next door" in a pretty dress. Ginny and I may not have been mincing along a street in New York but driving back down Princes Street would do very nicely as far as I was concerned. Romantic that I am part of me still thinks of her as the "girl next door". Although this doesn't mean, let me be quick to say, I don't also recognise a woman who knows what makes life tick, has her own point of view and doesn't mind letting you know what it is: the girl of my dreams.[19]

Edinburgh New Town *Shutterstock*

Life in the City

We have gone back to Travelodge for our Edinburgh stay and booked with the one in the New Town. The Georgian façade remains but inside the rooms have been reorganised to make for hotel bedrooms and one of them is ours. We are at the back so it's quiet and seems cosy and comfortable; you know what you'll get with Travelodge.

The New Town is an Edinburgh feature, created in the eighteenth century because the Old Town centred on The Mound was overcrowded. The Town Council under the leadership of the Provost, George Drummond, organised an architectural competition. The winning design would reflect the spirit of the Age of Enlightenment. It would seek to keep in the city the go-ahead residents who otherwise might beetle off to London. Some of the ungrateful, who should have known better, had already done just that and something had to be done. So, this was to be an upmarket development that would attract the well-to-do.

A 26-year-old James Craig came up with the goods and won the competition in 1766. His design was simple but effective. The new housing would lie to the north of the then city. There would be one main street, to be named George Street after the King, with Queen Street and Princes Street on the peripheries. It's always a good idea to keep in with the royal family of the day. Although, Princes Street was originally going to be St Giles Street, but the name was changed by the King after he discovered that St Giles, patron saint of the city, was also the patron saint of lepers, a bad omen.

The Union was a touchy area for some, even then, and so in an attempt to keep things together the two squares planned for the development were named St Andrew Square and St George Square, patron saints north and south. These in turn were linked by the monarch through George Street, which ran from one to the other, so symbolising the Union between Scotland and England. In a similar way there would also be Thistle Street and Rose Street: the emblems of the two countries.

At the time, the creation of the New Town was the largest planned city development in the world. After a slow start, when a discount was offered to builders willing to take it on, it proved to be a great success both commercially and aesthetically, and became known as "The Athens of the North".

This is still true today and New Town is an admired piece of Georgian architecture. As with our Travelodge many of the interiors have been adapted but walking the streets you still get a sense of the grandeur of it all and your spirits are lifted by the classical design and broad and open streets and pavements. This is true of much of central Edinburgh and it is for this reason a great city to visit and be part of, even if only for a short while.

Most people in the world now live in cities. They are not all designed with aesthetic appeal. There is much high rise, which doesn't suit everyone, and cities have a reputation for low life and aspects of human activity that don't bring out the best in people. There is an old adage that reinforces this: You are nearer to God in a garden than anywhere else on earth. This suggests that if you want to find God don't look in the city; best go to the countryside.

This view was challenged in the 1980s by the Archbishop of Canterbury's Commission report *Faith in the City*[20] and before that with the publication in 1975 of *Built as a City*[21] by David Sheppard, then Bishop of Woolwich. Both the Commission and the book took a long hard look at city and urban life. They examined both the role of the church and the state in the city and the city as a place where you might expect to find God. They saw that he is hidden in the city and often goes unrecognised, incognito, in the urban sprawl. Because the Church has its ear to the ground in local areas – it is after all usually made up of local people – it is in a good position to identify the hand of God in urban life and the needs of the people who live there.

Both the report and the book spoke to local and national authorities caught up in city life and their economic and political responsibilities. Some didn't like this because there are always those who think religion and politics don't mix. In contrast the writers could see that it was politics and economics which were critical in shaping people's lives. Both report and book came in for criticism and at times attack. Some thought that if there were problems for people living in cities what was needed was greater self-reliance. Black people living in the city were encouraged to not look for greater state support but to work themselves out of poverty, through self-education and respect for the police. These qualities are not to be dismissed but, as was later to emerge, black people didn't always see it that way and especially when it came to the police. It was the Macpherson Report[22], twenty years after *Faith in the City*, which described the police as "institutionally racist". Macpherson defined this as "The collective failure of an organisation to provide appropriate and professional service to people because of their colour, culture or ethnic origin".

There will always be those who individualise social issues and see the way out as being through personal endeavour. What each person can bring will be important but often the forces ranged against the individual are great and sometimes overwhelming. This is why those who pull the big strings politically and economically must be involved; social and economic policy will be a vital ingredient, and remedy.

The two Church reports challenged the state and the church to do better by urban areas. The city was a place where God was active. This could be seen not only in its architectural and artistic life, as in Edinburgh, but more especially and more to the point, in its economic and working life, in the building of communities and the enabling of people to fulfil their potential. Working class people often found that they didn't have a voice or access to pull the strings that made for change. Edinburgh New Town had been built for the rich and well-to-do of the day. The same level of energy and aspiration was needed towards ensuring that all those who lived in cities, not just those at the top of the social pecking order, could enjoy and benefit from the wealth and opportunities that were created there. When that happened, it was there that God would be seen to be at work. It was the work of the church and the state to enable that to take place.

In *Built as a City* David Sheppard tells the story of a group of forty or so local people in Canning Town, east London, where he had headed up a Family Centre and Community Church called The Mayflower. (It is here that Ginny and I met when we both worked there in a junior capacity.) An academic surgeon came to talk to this local group about the ethics of transplants, a topic current at the time. Sheppard thought perhaps three of the forty had passed their eleven-plus. The group put hard questions to the surgeon for over two hours. Afterwards he said he felt as exhausted as he would be by his most able students.

Sheppard cites this as both an example of how able ordinary working class people are and also how ability develops and flourishes when given the right opportunities to do so. The local church can play a key part in enabling that to happen. Real ability lies hidden in many people and is not realised. Christians believe that everyone is made in God's image and likeness and has innate ability waiting to be set free. This perspective is all part of the Church's mission to urban priority areas. We have to believe in people and stand with them and by them.

Things have moved on since the seventies and eighties and this story might almost now seem patronising. But it remains true that the opportunities everyone deserves are often thwarted by class or by being a member of a disadvantaged group or faith. This is why Christians will want to fight for the city to be a place where all those who live there benefit and not just the wealthy. We still place too high a regard on those who work with their heads and undervalue those who work with their hands, who in any case also work with their heads. There is too great a disparity between these groups in terms of how each is valued and therefore what each is paid. This is why Christians will also be concerned about economic and social policy and see it as part of their vocation to be involved with both.

Divergent groups in city life too often remain isolated from one another when they need to meet and understand what each brings to the table.

What *Built as a City* and the *Faith in the City* report highlight is how people are undervalued. This undervaluing includes the poor facilities and opportunities which are theirs by virtue of living in a city. Whereas, at their best, cities can be vibrant communities to grow up in. It is why you are as near to God in the city as you are in the countryside, or anywhere else on earth. It is why we should not hide God away in the countryside, present though he clearly is there (and the countryside has its own challenges), but see him as at the centre of city life. He is ready to shape it and respect it. His hidden hand is at work everywhere. What *Faith in the City* and *Built as a City* did was to address the challenges and point out the opportunities that are in the city today for both Church and state.

Local parish churches do best when they are fully engaged with the community they seek to serve; when they are at the centre of parish life. In the same way the Church as a national institution does best when it is fully engaged with the life of the nation. It will do that by its ethical concern as well as the services it offers for those important moments in life focused around birth, marriage and death. But it should not fight shy of engaging with the life of the nation socially, economically and politically as well. This is what *Faith in the City* achieved.

For a while it looked as if this might prove the last time the Church as an institution would seriously confront both itself, and those who hold secular power and influence over these policies, and the way they affect the lives of the people the Church seeks to serve. However, at the time of writing, it looks as though, under an initiative by the Archbishop of York, Stephen Cottrell, there may be Church Commissions in the pipeline which will address housing and other social issues of the day in much the same way as that taken by *Faith in the City*. This is a welcome development because it shows that the Church is still willing to grapple with those things which matter a great deal to ordinary people and shape their lives.

> Jesus Christ is raging, raging in the streets,
> Where injustice spirals and real hope retreats.
> Listen, Lord Jesus, I am angry too;
> In the kingdom's causes let me rage with you.[23]

El Greco: Christ Blessing (The Saviour of the World) National Gallery, Scotland[24]

El Greco face to face

Ginny has always loved the paintings of El Greco and it has sometimes been said that I am a beneficiary because my length and leanness chimed in with her admiration of his elongated figures. So when we are in Edinburgh we usually visit the Scottish National Gallery to see El Greco's *Christ Blessing*, also known as *The Saviour of the World*.[24] It was painted about 1600 and depicts a three-quarter-length image of Jesus, right hand raised in blessing, looking directly at you, eye to eye. He holds your gaze and El Greco's use of white paint conveys the idea of the divine so it is as though you are looking at God himself, which is exactly what traditional Christian theology teaches: Jesus is divine.

Some years ago, in the 1990s, we went to Toledo where El Greco lived and painted for more than thirty years until his death in 1614. It was also a kind of pilgrimage. We might have been in search of God, but we certainly were in search of El Greco. We discovered him in Toledo in a small out of the way church and at the time I wrote:

The Church of St Thomas takes some finding for first-time visitors. We hurry along when a notice indicates 50m to go, only to find it is 50m to the car park of the Church of St Thomas, which isn't at all the same thing. Other back alleys prove no more fruitful, but after some asking and pointing and gesticulating, in what Spanish we can muster, we find a small, unassuming church which has as its altarpiece one of the greatest of El Greco's paintings, 'The Burial of the Count Orgaz'. There is a modern narthex to the church, with souvenir shop and place to queue. On the steps an old woman in black and a child are begging; embarrassed, we hurry past. The queue is not long and for 150 pesetas you can enter what was once a church and is now an art gallery, with one painting. The church has been stripped of its religious artefacts, so that every eye is focused on the altarpiece still hanging where it was painted and intended by El Greco, and those who commissioned him. The lighting is subdued to protect and highlight the painting. We shuffle forward in the half-light to overhear an English commentary from the guide to one of the many parties to pass through that day. At the end the guide says, "Let's go", as they hurry off for their next encounter with great art for five minutes. Now it's our turn.

There is a constant stream of people pushing forward, eager to see this masterpiece. The pressure from new arrivals behind moves others forward and out of the church. We decide to linger and get a seat on the side where long wooden benches run at right angles to the sanctuary, although from here we can't actually see the painting, now hidden behind a pillar. The place for visitors to view is small and restricted.

In front of the painting a low metal rail keeps the crowd at bay. From where we sit we get a good view of the faces of the people as they come forward to the rail and get their chance to view the painting. Some are aghast and overawed, others point fingers with outstretched arms whispering explanations as they do so, others use binoculars to get in really close. We are now pinned in and the legs of those coming forward rub against ours, trapped as we are on the side benches.

This may no longer be a church, but these people are worshipping what they see before them. They display all the gestures and wonder of those who used to come here requesting their favourite saint's intercessions, and their prayers to God. Now the saint is an artist, and this has become a shrine to one of his paintings. Why is this painting of the burial of a long-forgotten nobleman of such magnitude?

The picture captures the tenderness of St Stephen and Augustine of Hippo as they cradle the body of the dead Count in their arms. The painting was commissioned by the parish priest of St Thomas, Andrés Núñez de Madrid, as an altar piece in the 16th century, and two centuries after the Count had died. The contract is dated 18 March 1586 and the work was to be finished by Christmas of that year. The Count was renowned for his generosity. He had funded local religious institutions like the Augustinian Convent of St Stephen. This painting commemorates just how much he was revered when alive, and how deserving of being received into heaven he was at his death.

In the lower part of the painting we see Stephen and Augustine with the Count in their arms. The legend was that they had both appeared at his funeral, lowering him into his tomb themselves. Then behind them come the heads of the benefactors in their white ruffs, who had actually paid for the painting. And then above them, and occupying the greater part of the canvas, is a vision of heaven, with Jesus at its pinnacle and Mary to one side. The soul of the Count is pictured as a baby being born in unhindered labour into an afterlife, and then taken up into heaven by Christ himself.

It is the striking humanity of this great painting which makes it so memorable and transfixing to those who come to see it. It pictures a community caring for its dead in a way we would all like to feel we will be treated and remembered at our own passing. The gentleness and concern is touching and compelling. The people who matter are gathered around. The parish priest is there, as are El Greco himself and his son, Jorge Manuel, who was then about eight years old; an Augustinian monk and a Franciscan friar; Peter with the keys of the Kingdom; John the Baptist; and the Holy Virgin. They are all gathered to receive one who seems youthful, albeit grey and already dead as they cradle him and receive him as their own. The colours are bright and filled with light and therefore hope. The figures, as always with El Greco, are elongated and their size and position related to their importance in the heavenly scheme of things. The whole effect is to promote a return to Catholicism in the face of challenges, not only from

Protestantism but also Islam and Judaism as well. This was all part of the religious and ethnic culture of the day and how they saw things and was at least partly the motivation behind the commission. If that was indeed the case, El Greco has succeeded also in giving the painting a universal appeal for all time. It speaks not only about the noble count, but also about any death – our death – and so it warms our hearts and draws us in.[25]

Western society is largely secular now but the need for sacred things remains. Sacred things are precious and hold our attention. Sometimes the trivial becomes sacred and is given an importance it doesn't merit. When it does it wears a hollow crown. The truly sacred, by contrast, still holds good in the best sense when what is sacred – a picture, a place, a piece of music – captures our humanity. This is why the life of Christ has in the past been the inspiration for so much great music and art and literature. What we see in him resonates with our own birth and suffering and dying. We reverence him because he brings his compassion to our aid. His empathy is expressed in what we see and hear and read about him so that these things become sacred because they say all that we feel. The truly world class images of the Christian tradition are: The Madonna and Child, The Crucifixion and The Pieta where Mary holds the body of Jesus taken down from the cross. At the feet of the sacred is where we lay our burden down and in that sacred moment reach out for a hand to lift us up and sustain us. God is with us and we tread on holy ground.

The drawing room on Britannia.

Britannia

As a final fling in Edinburgh and before returning home we decide to do the tour of the Royal Yacht *Britannia*, now moored permanently in Leith, the dockland area for the city. Like almost everything else in life, it seems, it is accessed at the end of a large shopping complex. We have booked tickets ahead, but we needn't have bothered because there is no queue and the number of visitors modest; we are out of season.

We get one of those audio commentaries you hold to the ear and away we go. The commentator is male and has a suitably deferential tone as he conducts you round this royal ship. We start on the bridge and you can sit in the very chair where only the captain was permitted when *Britannia* was up and running under steam. *Britannia* is an attractive ship and you can see why the Queen, if reported correctly, was reluctant to give her up and would miss being on board. This ship is large enough to sail the seven seas but small enough to remain intimate and friendly. Her keel was laid in 1952 and she was launched in 1953. Unsurprisingly she has a 1950s feel about her as you move round the cabins and decks. She may have been post-war but there was still an eye to austerity, as Britain recovered from wartime shortages. Despite this there is a sense of elegance and good taste from that period – Heals perhaps, but before Habitat.

Britannia was always the Queen's ship but she had a diplomatic role and she could, as well, be used as a hospital ship if the need arose. She played an important part in the evacuation of British nationals from Aden when civil war broke out in the Yemen in 1986. She was the Queen's ship because, as becomes clear on the tour, the ship was all about supporting the Queen on royal tours and trade missions promoting British industry and commerce around the world.

She carried 200 crew and 20 officers who, the commentary points out, had to stand to one side and pretend the Queen wasn't there should she pass by. The crew didn't wear hats as they would have needed to salute every time royalty came into view and then have the salute returned. Life could easily have deteriorated into a Monty Python sketch with saluting and standing up every few yards bringing life as we know it to a standstill.

On the tour you get to see the Queen's bedroom and Prince Philip's as well. They each have a single bed and there was no double bed on board until introduced by Prince Charles on his marriage to Diana. The bedrooms are modest if comfortable with no sense of grandeur: no drapes or crowns or four posters in view. It's hard to know where the single bedrooms tradition in royal circles comes from. All families and marriages do things in ways that work best for them. I am only too grateful to have a hand to hold in the wee small hours when dreams can be frightening and things go bump in the night.

Britannia was decommissioned in 1997 and you can see why. She needed attention to keep her running and given the number of crew and supporting cast she was expensive to maintain, too expensive for the New Labour government of the day. *Britannia* was useful and she enhanced monarchy. But it was, as so often in the modern era, a question of striking a note that sees the monarchy clothed in the right kind of dignity but in a way that means people feel the monarch is one of us. Not many of us have private yachts at our disposal and those that do tend to be out of favour with the population at large. *Britannia*, much loved as she was, had to go.

Part Five
Travelling Home
God invites us to make our home with him

" 'Tis dangerous to take a cold, to sleep, to drink; but I tell you, my lord fool, out of this nettle, danger, we pluck this flower, safety"
Shakespeare, Henry IV Part 1

The Flying Scotsman leaving York station bound for Waverley *Shutterstock*

Eleven: Back on track

We go to Waverley Station to catch the train on the east coast line to Kings Cross. Waverley is where Ginny arrived in the early sixties by steam on the *Flying Scotsman* when the family moved from Brighton. We have come to have a special affection for Waverley and all things Edinburgh, so in many ways it is a sad goodbye until we shall meet again. On the way south we will come to Durham where I spent a year at the end of the sixties as part of pre-ordination training. It was an eye opener, both in the liberal arts course which opened up the worlds of philosophy, art and literature, and in my seeing for the first time the cross section of traditions and personalities which make up Anglican clergy. The year's course was run from a college which served the C of E as a whole. Up until then I had grown up and been sheltered in Conservative Evangelical circles. This was a straight up and down world of collar and tie and polished shoes. But in Durham there were others from the Anglo-Catholic wing of Anglicanism; many were gay and many were camp. They had girls' names for each other and there was a good deal of "ooh... *she's* not really my type" and "who'd have believed it?", which owed quite a lot to Frankie Howerd. I began to see there was more to the Church of England than meets the eye, or had met mine at least.

Train buffs

All this was before we were married. Ginny used to come up to Durham on the milk train from London which arrived about 3am. This was in the days of single compartments with one long seat down either side. In the middle of the night, when sleep couldn't be resisted any longer, passengers either ended up sprawled full length, if there was room, or nodding off on the shoulder of a complete stranger. I would meet Ginny and see her to a B and B until a more respectable hour.

It was 1970. Simon and Garfunkel brought out *Bridge Over Troubled Water* that year and we bought our copy of the then vinyl LP in Durham. We had nothing to play it on but Ginny took it back to London and turned up the volume on her record player. The title track is reminiscent of Carole King's *You've got a Friend* which was on her *Tapestry* album and released about the same time. It was a big hit for James Taylor. Both songs are about going the extra mile and reaching out in love and friendship when times is hard. They are love songs and just what we aspired to. All of which means that looking back now nostalgia is much in the air as we arrive at Durham. These songs represent romantic miles stones on the life and love we have shared together. In theory I don't do nostalgia but memories of being young and being in love aren't going to let theory get in the way and there is much tugging of the heart strings. Of course there was agonising then too but all that is forgotten now and instead I get a tear in the eye and a glow in the heart when I hear:

When you're weary, Feeling small
When tears are in your eyes
I'll dry them all,
I'm on your side
Oh, when times get rough
And friends just can't be found

Like a bridge over troubled water
I will lay me down
Like a bridge over troubled water
I will lay me down

Hornby Dublo: The perfect table top model railway

Coming into Durham by train from the south is a bit like having the curtain drawn back at the theatre and seeing the set for the first time. The track is screened, all is hidden, and then suddenly there are the Cathedral and the Castle, and you feel applause coming on for this northern set piece. There is a magnificence to both these buildings. If you live in Durham City they physically dominate your life and you couldn't but be influenced by being near them. They are reminders of divine and civic presence built by those who wanted to give glory to God and defend their territory.

So we settle into our seats heading south and wait for the glories of Durham to open up to us once again. If this has been a trip where we have discovered something of the past and its history, it has also been one which has revelled in the enjoyment there is to be had from travel by train. Before we set out none of what we have uncovered was known to us. But happily, there were many Durham moments where the curtain was drawn back to surprise us with new encounters. It's a bit like falling in love when everything is transformed by being together with the person of your dreams and you can't believe this can actually be happening to you. You discover another and life takes on a glow and a joy like nothing else. It doesn't go on like this indefinitely, of course, but it gets you going in every sense and while it lasts it lifts the spirit and quickens the heart. The journey we have made has done the same. There is a joy to be had in discovering people and places. It's all part of being in love with life, sharing an adventure with someone you care about and who just might be the person of your dreams. Travelling encapsulates all this. It has been life affirming. It has steered us away from the darkness that sometimes closes in and replaced it with a sense of contentment and being at our ease. Train travel has a lot to commend it, we decide.

Trains are a bit of a preoccupation with Anglican clergy. Eric Treacy was Bishop of Wakefield but he is remembered most for his love of all things to do with trains and railways. His photographic collection is now in the National Rail Museum at York. He had the distinction of dying of a heart attack on Appleby Station on the Settle to Carlisle line which, as all true train buffs know, is a jewel in the crown of British train journeys. I will put up my hand for being one of this (some might think) sad bunch of clergy. For me it's visits to heritage railways but also model railways. This is centred on collecting the vintage Hornby Dublo of my childhood which Hornby marketed as "the perfect table top railway". The glories of printed tin plate are not to be sniffed at and more than a cut above all things plastic which came later. Looking today at the attention to detail on the Hornby Dublo models brings back early memories laid out on many a dining room table in the 1950s. I belong to the Hornby Railway Collectors' Association and helped to start a local group. The group meets to run trains on carefully constructed layouts using original track as well as indulge in small talk about all things to do with Binns Road, Liverpool, where Hornby had their factory and Frank Hornby reigned supreme.

Possibly the best known of clergy mad about trains is the Revd Wilbert Awdry and the stories he wrote for children about Thomas the Tank Engine and James and Henry and all the others. I knew Mr Awdry's cousin Mick and his wife Anna when we lived in the same village they did, where I was Vicar, on the Surrey–Hampshire border. Mick and Anna were just as you would want them to be. They were absorbed in the immediate things of domestic life, cooking and repairing, their garden and the village where we lived. They came to church because they were conscious of a hidden presence in their lives which would guide them safe home when the time came. They were big-hearted and the kind of people you are just glad to have known and spent time with. Happily you meet people like Mick and Anna on train journeys. We have met them on ours and it's what has made the trip worthwhile.

Hidden people

If train travel is a gateway to falling in love with life it also allows you to watch the world go by; to be free from the normal everyday duties that crowd in all too easily and to enjoy that freedom for its own sake. That is one of the attractions of travel, it gets you out of a routine that easily pegs you down. Travel cuts you enough slack to be more available to yourself, and more available to other people.

The best in others often lies hidden from view and so to sit and unravel together is where the pleasure lies, them in the telling and sometimes the relief of getting it off their chest, and you, the listener, in responding and the rapport between you. This is not a licence for old bores to self-indulgently go on and on about themselves. It is at its best when the modest and unassuming can be coaxed into sharing their journey, allowing you a glimpse of what has transpired and lies closest to their heart. Some of that has gone on in this journey we have made to the Scottish west coast. We have discovered the places and people, contemporary and historical, that have brought that community to the present day. This discovery has been revealed in the not much more than passing glances we have been able to give in the time available. We have not plumbed the depths of the west of Scotland but it has been enough to paint a picture, and open a door, into a world rich and rare that would otherwise have lain hidden. We are grateful for that and it brings its own sense of contentment and completion as our journey comes to an end.

So that the last section of this book is not so much more of the journey we have made but a reflection on a journey which is to come and we all must make at the end of our lives. We live in the present and in many ways for the present. What does that future hold and what can we realistically and hopefully lay claim to and look forward to?

Twelve: Past, Present and Future

Present Tense

Your Holy hearsay
is not evidence:
Give me the good news
in the present tense

What happened
nineteen hundred years ago
May not have happened:
How am I to know?

The living truth
is what I long to see:
I cannot lean upon
what used to be

So shut the Bible up
and show me how
The Christ you talk about
Is living now.

Sydney Carter
(1915-2004)[26]

Trains take you to places and people, but they also take you home. It's where we're heading via Kings Cross. Home is where the heart is and where you long to be. In bleak moments I sometimes think of those who died in extreme and desperate situations, far from home. In wartime: in the First World War, Edith Cavell the British nurse in Belgium waiting to be shot as a spy for caring for wounded British and German soldiers alike; in the Second, Dietrich Bonhoeffer the German pastor, imprisoned for his opposition to the Third Reich and hanged agonisingly close to the end of the war for being in the know about the July plot to assassinate Hitler. How they must have longed to be home with those they loved and who loved them, to be in a place where all was safe and everyday. If only they could be home all would be well. It is their isolation and bleakness which resonates with my sometimes low mood; a mental image which captures my circumstances, trivial though they are compared with theirs. This is often triggered by something immediate, a bereavement or tragedy or failure, but it brings death and the dread of dying into plain view. These seem to be around more in later life, I've discovered, flapping about like the old black crows in the ash tree at the bottom of our garden.

Dying to live

Dying is sometimes referred to as going home. Old-time gospel songs take up that theme and invite you to get on board the gospel train which is bound for glory. Being with someone who has died has always pulled me in two directions. There is in a dead person an absolute stillness, no flicker of life to be found or detected. In his novel *Love over Scotland* Alexander McCall Smith gives that moment its own kind of beauty. One of the characters in the novel is Angus Lordie, a portrait painter. He has the unfortunate experience of having one of his clients die in front of him whilst sitting for Angus to paint his portrait. Angus writes to a friend to tell her what has happened. He puts it like this:

> *It was very peaceful, almost as if somebody had silently gone away, somewhere else, had left the room. How strange is the human body in death – so still, and so vacated. That vitality, that spark, which makes for life, is simply not there. The tiny movements of the muscles, the sense of there being somebody keeping the whole physical entity orchestrated in space – that goes so utterly and completely. It is no longer there.*[27]

Part of me asks can there be anything else beyond this. We are contained within this body and when the body comes to the end of its strength to live, that is the end of things, face up to it. Put away this romantic hope that there is "a home in glory land way beyond the blue". In any case who wants to live for ever? There needs to be an ending, a completion, as there was a beginning.

And yet, and yet, the stillness of those who have died speaks in another way. This person whom you have known is no longer present: "they have silently gone away, somewhere else... left the room". There is a body but the person you have loved is not there. So, where are they? The possibility of there being another life in another dimension comes into view. A place of gathering where love is shared; where a welcome awaits, friendship is renewed and loved ones embraced. A hidden hoped for. Is that possible?

The in-between land

When we come to try and reconcile the contradiction there is between hopeless cold death and hoped-for new life we find ourselves in a kind of in-between land, the land between earth and heaven. It is a land occupied by both hard-nosed pragmatism and sensitive spiritual awareness. There is more to life, and death, than meets the eye. The Christian tradition's understanding of what more there is can be found in the Bible and in the New Testament in particular.

In what follows I try to do justice to what those who came before us have testified to but to also take seriously my own present experience. In this I am on board with Sydney Carter and his poem *Present Tense* but I am not ready to throw the baby out with the bathwater. The New Testament accounts of the Resurrection of Jesus are the lynch-pin which holds the Christian story together. They can't be shelved without undermining what has been central to many lives and societies for two thousand years. The historical accounts and the "living truth" both matter. The question is can they be held together? Can we find enough in our present experience, in the living truth, to support and affirm the historic accounts of resurrection we find in the Bible. It's a big ask but let's see where the present and the past take us as we head for home.

It is faith which seeks to hold both doubt and hope in creative tension. Faith is not blind certainty; it is a dynamic relationship of the human and the divine. Faith is active and searching. Another word for faith is trust. Faith is trusting God in a way that enables us to articulate every doubt and question we have ever thought of and, at the same time, not ceasing to have God in our hearts, as our guiding light and inspiration. It isn't either/or, because faith holds *both*. That's what faith is; it is living with contradiction and not being thrown by it. God isn't a dictator unable to tolerate any kind of questioning or protest. He isn't looking for lip service. Instead he knows that wrestling with doubt and disbelief is the road that leads to truth, a crucible from which something richer will flow. It is also the road to hope. What we need when despair stalks our path, more than anything else, is hope. There are a couple of areas of our present experience which are the "living truth" and just might get us over the line when it comes to life after death. But first a look at just what the Bible does say when it comes to the Resurrection of Jesus.

The Gospel story

The Resurrection of Jesus is central to the Christian story. It is at the heart of Christian faith and holds the whole thing together. However, in the telling it is not as clear cut as may first appear and some would like us to believe.

The disciples found themselves in the in-between land after the Crucifixion of Jesus had taken place. He was taken down from the cross. His legs were not broken to hasten death, as was sometimes the case, he was already dead, let there be no doubt, and he was placed in a new tomb in which no one had ever been laid. A stone was rolled across the door and that was that.

But then in St Mark's Gospel we read: "When the sabbath was over, Mary of Magdala, Mary the mother of James, and Salome bought aromatic oils, intending to go and anoint Jesus".[28] But their intention was frustrated, the tomb was empty; the body gone, the stone had been removed. It was from that moment that it became clear, according to the gospel accounts, that Jesus had risen from the grave. The gospels are in no doubt about this either. It is not written down blatantly by the gospel writers but is a simple retelling of what happened.

However, there is a veil which hides from view the exact details and that's why there is something enigmatic about it all. The gospel accounts of the Resurrection need to be read carefully. They ask anyone who reads them to make up his or her mind about just what they think took place.

In the Resurrection story, as the writers tell it, Jesus seems to be sometimes present in human form, just as the disciples saw him before the Crucifixion. He eats breakfast with them and talks one to one. He walks the earth like he always did. But in contrast sometimes his presence seems to be ethereal: he passes through closed doors and into locked rooms. On yet other occasions, he seems to be hidden and disguised. He shows himself to two disciples walking to the village of Emmaus but they don't recognise him. It is only later when he breaks bread with them, in a house in the village itself, that the penny drops and they know it's him but then he mysteriously disappears from their sight. In a similar way he appears to Mary of Magdala when she comes to visit the tomb of Jesus, but she too fails to recognise him and thinks he is the gardener. It is only when he speaks her name that she knows it's him. The writers, Luke and John, emphasise the action of breaking bread and the speaking of a name as the ways in which God discloses himself to his disciples. Their message is that it happened then and it happens now.

So what appears to be the case is that there is a hiddenness in these accounts which can't be avoided. It is not clear exactly what did happen and what the disciples actually saw. The veil is lifted but not completely. This is not the kind of evidence you might expect to be given in a court of law by, for example, eyewitnesses to a road accident. Or perhaps it is, in that each writer has their own take and reports from their perspective on what took place. It is said that eyewitness accounts of the same incident often differ greatly because each sees it from their own point of view. That is exactly the case when it comes to the New Testament accounts of the post-Resurrection appearances of Jesus. What we can say is that what the gospel writers want to convey is that Jesus had overcome death and they had seen him with their own eyes. This is their way of doing it. They use their imaginations to do so and present these different takes on what occurred.

Commenting on Mark's Gospel, and his understanding of the Resurrection, Richard Burridge draws out the enigmatic nature of Mark's narrative: "Like so much of his gospel, Mark's ending is full of enigma, fear and awe. Instead of tying things up with a nice, happy ending, this story just leaves us with more questions." And "Mark's narrative as we have it now ends as abruptly as it began. There was no introduction or background to Jesus' arrival, and none for his departure. No one knew where he came from; no one knows where he has gone; and not many understood him when he was here – an enigmatic figure whose power was realised in suffering and whose kingship was proclaimed in death."[29]

Sometimes the gospel writers seem to speak literally, sometimes they speak metaphorically. What they are certain of is that Jesus survived death and that there was for him, and so for us, a life beyond the grave. This is the point they want to get across. They use metaphor and story and paradox to do so. For those who know only too well the contradiction there is in living in the in-between land, the gospel stories, enigmatic though they may be, offer a foundation on which to build. This is what the Christian faith has held centre stage since the first century. So the question now is does our present experience back this up and add credibility to the traditional teaching we have received?

Using our imaginations

Sydney Carter is right in wanting the present to speak and for there to be an encounter with the divine and sacred in the present moment. This is particularly true when it comes to dying. We need God to be with us and to know he's there, of course we do. Death is a kind of despair when we see it only as a bleak ending so that when despair has us by the throat what we long for and look for, above all else, is hope. It is God who gives us the creative imagination to find hope in death and adversity. Hope is what comes out of despair. Looked at positively despair is the trigger. It is imagination which helps us see what faith can mean and can be for us when darkness falls. Imagination used to rate more highly than it does today for shedding light on what may or may not be true. The gospel writers used their imaginations to speak about the Resurrection but they are not alone.

In the medieval period people had no ready access to the Bible because many could not read, it was only available in Latin and printing was in its infancy. They knew the Bible stories because they were passed on by word of mouth and could often be found in picture form painted on the walls inside churches: Look – the Crucifixion, Look – the Resurrection. These stories and paintings were works of the imagination and were a stimulus to letting imagination have full rein in those who saw them. Those church wall paintings sometimes included other figures – ghost and ghouls – symbolising our inner doubts and fears. In this imaginative way the artist demonstrated the greatness of the Resurrection in overcoming our despair and giving us new life.

It is the arts that show us how far imagination can take us. Creative artists like painters, musicians and writers all use their imaginations. When they do so they often give voice to our deeper feelings about the lives we live and share together, and sometimes about God: the inner contentment in the smile on the *Mona Lisa* by Leonardo da Vinci; the inner agony in *The Scream* by Edvard Munch; the sense of the divine in *The Saviour of the World* by El

Greco as we saw in Edinburgh. Wendell Berry, the farmer poet, in what is probably his best-known poem, *The Peace of Wild Things*, describes how he finds peace in nature and the natural world "When despair for the world grows in me".[30] All these are works of the imagination and bring a new depth of expression to human experience.

It was this spiritual clothing that the medieval mystics like Julian of Norwich wrote about. Julian was probably the first woman to write a book in English, albeit the middle English of her day. She begins her *Revelations of the Divine Love* by recounting her own near death experience when she was in her thirties. She thought she was dying. The parish priest had been sent for; her body had become set but she survived and lived on. Out of this came her "showings" or visions of the Passion of Jesus which sprang from her imagination. She writes of death; she knows it well. Allowing her imagination full flow she brings hope and sheds new light on the Passion.

She does this by disclosing her own interior life and convictions. She brings us a new language and imagery to speak about God. She puts God's love at the centre of the Passion and so at the centre of dying. She addresses God as Mother. For her in God there is no anger. When in our sight we fall and fail God lifts us up and refuses to turn away. There is no finger of guilt pointing our way. In the face of death it is God who has all we shall ever need. In doing this she clothes God in a new rich apparel in which we can share. Because of her the faith we hold to has a spring in its step. When God is seen in a new light so are we. We will feel differently about ourselves because we feel differently about him. All this is a product of divinely inspired imagination and where it can take us. Her writings have been an immense source of hope and strength to many who, like her, are on a spiritual quest.

Not everything we imagine is real or can be brought into being. But when we look for a life to come, a home in heaven, it is our imagination that gives direction. It extends our understanding and we begin to see new possibilities. We begin to see that sometimes our dreams can come true. That's why imagination must be taken seriously and is a tool we use to find hope in the world. When we are overtaken by despair or laid low in adversity it is imagination that gets to work and looks for a way through, a way forward. Perhaps after all death is not the end but a beginning, perhaps after all despair doesn't need to rule the day but hope has real substance and is within our grasp.

Imagination beavers away. It doesn't throw up hands in horror but seeks to make sense of what we know. It pushes the boundaries of science. It understands that when we long for something it is because there is a real need with a real answer waiting to be discovered. When the need exists it's imagination that will find an answer. That's where hope lies. It is why the Resurrection story has such a strong appeal. It speaks to the depth of our need and suggests that a life to come is possible, just as we imagine. Imagination brings life after death into view and places it within our grasp.

We can't know exactly what such a life would be like. But looked at imaginatively it is possible to see that a time may come when clear thinking science and big-hearted faith can both believe an afterlife is possible, just as the gospel writers described it.

Saying our prayers

Faith looks back to the gospel stories, as solid ground on which to stand, and within, to draw on our imaginations. It also reaches out. It does so in prayer. The conundrum which living in the in-between land presents urges us on and wants us to explore further and go deeper. It is a conundrum which asks us to pray because in prayer we make contact with God. Prayer is another part of our living and present experience that helps us to have a grasp of hope beyond death.

In many world faiths God is personal and this is certainly true in the Christian tradition. What we do in prayer is to bring to God all that we are and all that we feel, and trust him with it. There will be days when the heavens are brass, and God seems remote and beyond our reach. But there will too be times when we know ourselves to have touched the hem of the divine, so immediate and real does prayer seem to be, and God within it. It verifies our trust and restores hope to our hearts. It makes believing in a life to come seem credible.

People's experience of prayer varies a great deal. Prayer takes various forms. Some will touch that divine hem through ecstatic utterance, others through dance and song and exuberance. For yet others the route, the journey of travel, is through contemplation and silence, by mantra repeated on the breath, perhaps even by being lost in thought gazing from a train window. The door of heaven is opened in prayer when we visit a sacred place; become absorbed in a much-loved picture; make a pilgrimage; listen to a piece of music; go to wild places that bring their own peace. It is in those moments we know we are not alone, that we are held by our right hand (Psalm 63) and that we are sheltered under the shadow of God's wing like a hen shelters her chicks (Psalm 91 and Matthew 23:37). What all these experiences of prayer give is a sense of God's presence and a peace of heart and mind. We know ourselves to be centred and focused in him. Prayer is knowing God, knowing him to be real and in our experience.

If there are various forms of prayer there are too different types of prayer. There are prayers of thanksgiving and of adoration; there are prayers of petition when we pray for ourselves and there are prayers of intercession when we pray for other people and situations. Not everyone is good at all these types of prayer. I don't find myself fluent in intercession and especially value those who can put into words what I want to say and ask.

For me God is most real in the stillness and in the silence of contemplative prayer. No need to say much, words get in the way, better to hold God in your heart and to know that you are there with him and it is enough. The affirming nature of prayer in the present tense requires us to take time and space to be alone with God. It is as though we are sitting by a quiet stretch of water or watching the sun slowly sinking below the horizon. There is in these moments a stillness which quietens our hearts and lets God be God for us. The focus is on God and not on us. The Spanish mystic St John of the Cross describes his own experience in prayer by using the natural world as a metaphor of his encounter and experience of God, the Beloved.

My Beloved is the mountains,
The solitary wooded valleys,
The strange islands,
The raging torrents,
The whisper of the amorous breezes.

The tranquil night
At the approaches of dawn.
The silent music,
The murmuring solitude,
The supper that revives and enkindles love.

It is knowing God in these ways that will give us the reassurance that death is no barrier and the God who is here now will be there then.

To pray contemplatively many people use a mantra such as "Lord have mercy" or a single word like "Father" or the Jesus Prayer "Lord Jesus Christ, Son of God, have mercy upon me". When repeated slowly on the breath a mantra brings us into the presence of God and creates a oneness in our heart with him. He is there with us; a nearness which is both compelling an affirming.

In prayer we know we have been with God. We have an inner sense that we are with him and he with us. Prayer is how we reach and make contact with God. It is in prayer he knows us by name and he holds us in his heart. The God who we know now in the present tense and in the present moment is the same God who brought Jesus back from the dead. Here is the living truth that resurrection is possible and we can be part of it.

Talking and Listening

It's no good going it alone. If the gospel story and imagination and prayer play their part in how we see death and how we cope with despair, so too does being with other people. We are community. We are meant to be together. We don't do well to keep all that we feel and question and hope for locked up inside us. We do well when we share and disclose.

This means that we can openly discuss how we read the gospel stories, where our imaginations lead us and what we experience in prayer. We can say how much we are fearful of dying, or being ill, or some other monster of the night that hovers over us. In that way we also get a different kind of perspective. It is to receive the affirmation and support from other people which giving and receiving love brings. It is to find a fellow traveller in the in-between land and to know we are not the only one as we speak and listen together. So don't close down or bottle up but talk and share and join hands. We are all on the same journey and do best when we march with others shoulder to shoulder and arm in arm. It is in this way that death need no longer be dreaded and despair can be wrapped up and put away. We travel hopefully when we travel in good company. It all becomes part of our present experience confirming the gospel story in the present tense.

Faith in action

On Change of Weathers

And were it for thy profit, to obtaine
All *Sunshine*? No vicissitude of *Raine*?
Thinkst thou, that thy laborious Plough requires
Not Winter *frosts*, as well as Summer *fiers*?
There must be both: Sometimes these hearts of ours
Must have the sweet, the seasonable Showers
Of *Teares*; Sometimes the Frost of chill *despaire*
Makes our desired *sunshine* seeme more faire:
Weathers that most oppose the Flesh and Blood,
Are such as helpe to make our *Harvest* good:
We may not choose, great God: It is thy *Task*:
We know not what to *have*; nor how to ask.

Francis Quarles
English poet (1592-1644)[31]

Faith isn't whistling in the dark, when chill despair and death are close at hand, neither is it denial of the doubts and the uncertainty we often feel. We move forward in our frailty taking these with us as we reach out to discover God and life more fully and completely. He doesn't look for blind allegiance but honesty and integrity of life. We reach into the hiddenness which is God and about whom there will always be mystery. Faith leads us out of darkness into a place where light is breaking. It is not knowing everything about the divine, how could you, but sensing his transcendence and his greatness, his intimacy and his love of small things and each living person; it is a journey, a process, a relationship, an ongoing conversation. It is "Winter frosts, as well as Summer fiers".

Faith is trusting; we don't have all the answers but are happy in our not knowing. We see into a world which transcends the immediate and lifts us beyond ourselves. It doesn't matter that we have not nailed everything down. It matters that we are searching with God by our side. Faith is a way of knowing. It is like knowing you are in love. There is a knowing which goes deeper than seeing. It is knowing in your soul and in the depth of your being. It is knowing we are not alone but held by God's hand. We know him in humility and not in arrogance. It is knowing there is much we do not know.

I was once a member of an amateur street theatre group called The Clowns. Each of us took on the persona of a circus clown of one sort or another. We didn't have many scripts but the one we did most was a presentation of the Crucifixion. This wasn't surprising as we were all training to be ordained and went on into full time ministry. Portraying Jesus as a clown was familiar enough. About the same time he had appeared in this way in the musical *Godspell* so this was our take on an old theme. There was a good deal of slapstick and knockabout but the pathos of the innocent fool picked on by others and finally hung on a cross was telling. To see Jesus as a clown runs the risk of making him a trivial figure. What is meant is not this but instead that the hope we look for has a foolishness about it because it seems so out of reach and unlikely and against self interest.

How can Jesus as a social outcast who dies on a cross, a sign of humiliation, bring hope to the world? Clowns are immensely sympathetic figures and what they bring into view, in their innocence, is his humanity. When Jesus is seen as the clown, or the fool, he identifies with those who suffer and are broken and he is able to do so because he has been down that road himself, foolish though it was to go there. This is where our hope lies, in the foolishness of one who laid down his life and forgave even those who took that life away. It is just this kind of selflessness that brings hope to the world but which the world laughs at. The foolishness we see in Jesus is exactly where his greatness and strength lies. His kingship is seen not in the exercise of power but in his willingness to lay down his life and therefore to stand in solidarity with all who suffer.

In a similar way this is what we saw in Greta Thunberg, a foolish school girl, when she displayed a wisdom that put the adult world to shame. We saw it in all those who were fools to themselves in the Covid pandemic. They went on caring and going into schools and hospitals and care homes even though they knew the risk of going there. It was the NHS and front line workers who brought hope to many people and that's why the Thursday evening clapping told its own story. In two world wars we saw it in all those who laid down their lives like Edith Cavell and Dietrich Bonhoeffer. Foolish all these may have been but they were the hope the world badly needed. They knew there was a deeper meaning and purpose to life and this was the only sure ground to stand on. It spelt out plainly and boldly, and yet in an unassuming way, where true greatness lies – in loving your neighbour as yourself, in loving God and believing in God with all your heart and with all your soul and with all your mind. They were humanity at its best and it knocked for six self-seeking and being ego-centred and getting rich and all the other hollow crowns we may grasp for and seek to wear.

If that is hope in this life, hope in a life yet to come is another kind of foolishness. Although there is evidence of life after death and reason to believe, as I have tried to show, in the end it will always be a matter of faith. It can never be beyond doubt but instead something taken on trust. Those who hold that belief in their hearts will be seen by many as foolish daydreamers. St Paul put it into words when he wrote: "We are fools for Christ's sake".[32] But it's for real. It is hope for the world. It is here we nail our colours to the mast and here we make our stand.

When it comes to life after death foolish we may be to believe in it but it is belief out of our present experience and in the present tense. Knowing Christ in the present brings its own reassurance. The one who is with us now will be with us, and we with him, in the hereafter and all will be well. This is based on the evidence of the Bible's account of Jesus' Resurrection but it also springs from imagination and is wrapped in prayer. Fools we may be but we know now where our hope lies: in this life, as best we can, by laying down our lives in ways small and sometimes great, and at the same time daring to believe that this life is but a preparation for a life yet to come.

Heaven in ordinary

And so we are nearly home after our Scottish journey that turned into a pilgrimage. The local suburban stopping train takes us on the last leg. When we arrive there is no banging the door this time but a key in the lock and pushing the post on the mat to one side as the door opens. We didn't leave the oven on and everything looks pretty much as it was. It's great to be back. It's a relief. We were glad to go. We enjoyed the trip but now we are home with all that is familiar and just as it should be. The happiness of the family home in Nazareth and the warmth of the manger in Bethlehem come into view.

Perhaps that's how it will be when life comes to an end. Life was the journey, the pilgrimage, and we are thankful for all we received and enjoyed: the frosts, the fiers and the sunshine. But now we have reached a home in heaven and it is the homely and familiar which bring their own happiness. Heaven in ordinary. I was never much convinced or attracted by choirs of angels singing their heads off or that blinding unapproachable light. Instead I will be quite content to find it is a question of settling down and being at ease with myself and with God. Home is where the heart is and my heart is at home with the ordinary and familiar.

"Ah. Hello. Come in, you're very welcome, have a seat. Can I get you anything? Make yourself at home."

The Adoration of the Shepherds[33]

Would you know your Lord's meaning in this?
Learn it well. Love was his meaning.
Julian of Norwich[34]

O come, thou Dayspring, come and cheer
our spirits by thine advent here;
disperse the gloomy clouds of night
and death's dark shadows put to flight.[35]

Bibliography

Quotations, Sources and Permissions

1. Laurie Lee, *As I Walked Out One Midsummer Morning*, Penguin, 1971
2. St John's Gospel, 11:33–6 (AV)
3. *The Train to Glasgow* by Wilma Horsbrugh published by The Albion Press 2004. I have tried to establish the Copyright holder for this poem but I am sorry to say I have been unsuccessful. I reprint in part under Section 30 of Copyright, Designs and Patents Act 1998.
4. Julian of Norwich, *Revelations of Divine Love*, Penguin, 1966
5. Quoted by Norrie Gilliland in *Glasgow's Forgotten Village*, published in 2002 (ISBN 0-9542764-0-X), which gives a full and comprehensive account of how Grahamston was taken over and transformed by the coming of the railway into Glasgow.
   See the website: www.grahamston.com
6. A. Causey, "Stanley Spencer and the Art of his Time", quoted by Keith Bell in *Stanley Spencer*, Phaidon Press, 1992
7. Julian of Norwich *Revelations of Divine Love*, Penguin, 1966
8. For further information published by "Faith in Cowal" see their website: www.faithincowal.org. The historical paper and supporting illustrations were prepared by Bob Reid, are on the Campbell Clan website and are copyright Robert Reid. The photographs of St Munn and Holy Loch were taken by Daniel Romani and also appear on the "Faith in Cowal" website and are used here with his permission.
9. Prospero in *The Tempest* by William Shakespeare

9a James Rebanks, *English Pastoral*, Penguin Books 2020

10. David Scott, "Skellig St Michael: A Pilgrimage", from *Beyond the Drift: New and Selected Poems*, Bloodaxe Books, 2015, with permission. www.bloodaxebooks.com.

11. Rosemary Fletcher Blog; https://www.persabus.co.uk/blo
With permission

12. I sourced the information for this section, with permission, from Mairead Mackechnie, *The Lord of the Isles,* The Finlaggan Trust, 2018

13. The Book of Ruth, 1:1, 3, 4, 8, 14–18 (REB, adapted)

14. St Luke's Gospel, 10:28–37 – the Good Samaritan (REB)

15. St Luke's Gospel, 22:24–7 (REB)

16. Lavinia Byrne, *The Rhythm of the Hours*, Hodder and Stoughton, 2001

17. Wikipedia: The Caledonian Canal

18. Galatians, 3:26–8 (NEB)

19. Bob Dylan *The Freewheelin' Bob Dylan*, 1963 CBS

20. The Archbishop of Canterbury's Commission on Urban Priority Areas, *Faith in the City*, 1985

21. David Sheppard, *Built as a City*, Hodder and Stoughton, 1974

22. Sir William Macpherson, *The Stephen Lawrence Inquiry*, 1999: report of the Inquiry into the death of Stephen Lawrence and the police investigation which followed.

23. From the hymn "Justice is waiting" by John Bell and Graham Maule in "Ancient and Modern" published by Hymns Ancient and Modern Ltd 2013 with permission.

24. El Greco, *Christ Blessing* or *The Saviour of the World* (circa 1600), in The Scottish National Gallery and reproduced with permission of The National Galleries of Scotland

25. David Eaton, *I'm Not a Great Lover of Vicars*, Way House Books, 2012

26. Sydney Carter, *Present Tense*, from *Songs of Sydney Carter*, a CD made for his 1971 Australian Tour which may be downloaded from iTunes Music Store or streamed from Apple Music. It is also available on YouTube. With permission from Stainer and Bell Ltd.

27. Alexander McCall Smith, *Love Over Scotland*, Abacus, 2006

28. St Mark's Gospel, 16:1 (REB)

29. Richard Burridge, *Four Gospels, One Jesus? A symbolic reading*, SPCK, 1994, pp. 63–5

30. Wendell Berry, "The Peace of Wild Things", in *The Peace of Wild Things and other poems*, Penguin, 2018

31. This text is made available under a Creative Commons Compatible Licence

32. I Corinthians, 4:10 (REB)

33. Gerard van Honthorst, *Adoration of the Shepherds* (1622), Wallraf-Richartz Museum, Cologne, reproduced with permission

34. Julian of Norwich, *Revelations of Divine Love*, Penguin, 1966

35. "O come, O come, Emmanuel", Latin Advent antiphon, translated by J. M. Neale (alt.), *Ancient and Modern*, Hymns Ancient and Modern Ltd, 2013. Out of copyright.

All photographs are by David and Ginny Eaton unless otherwise attributed.